– Updated & Enlarged Second Edition –

ALFA ROMEO

GIULIA
Coupé GT & GTA

First published in 1992 by Veloce Publishing Limited, 33 Trinity Street, Dorchester DT1 1TT, England. Reprinted 1996, 1998. This updated and revised second edition published in 2003. Reprinted 2004 & May 2007. Fax 01305 268864/e-mail info@veloce.co.uk/web www.veloce.co.uk or www.velocebooks.com
ISBN 978-1-906706-47-0/UPC 6-36847-00247-3

Readers with ideas for automotive books, or books on other transport or related hobby subjects, are invited to write to the editorial director of Veloce Publishing at the above address.
British Library Cataloguing in Publication Data - A catalogue record for this book is available from the British Library.
Typesetting, design and page make-up all by Veloce Publishing on Apple Mac. Printed in Italy by Grafiche Flaminia.

– Updated & Enlarged Second Edition –

ALFA ROMEO

GIULIA
Coupé GT & GTA

– John Tipler –

VELOCE PUBLISHING
THE PUBLISHER OF FINE AUTOMOTIVE BOOKS

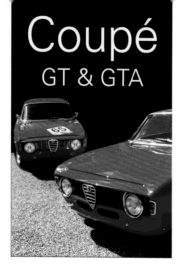

Acknowledgements

Very many thanks to everyone who has helped me produce this book, especially Jon Dooley, who guided me through his extensive archives, giving technical and historical advice as well as lending pictures and brochures; Tim Stewart of Huntsworth Garage and Richard Banks for their insight into the Giulia market; Chris Sweetapple, keeper of the Giulia 105 Register, for photographs and his knowledge of detail changes in Giulia development; Michael Lindsay for pictures and background on the AROC; Richard Gadeselli of Fiat, who obtained archive pictures and data; Rhoddy Harvey Bailey for his reminiscences of the Autodelta days; Andrea de Adamich for the Foreword, and his secretary Casandra Pappas for liaison; Dott. Ing. Carlo Chiti for details about Autodelta; Malcolm Morris for describing the restoration process; Alan Lis for recent competition history; Laurie Caddell and Pete Robain for some excellent transparencies; Annice Collett at the National Motor Museum; Charles Pierce for assistance with pictures; *Road & Track* and *Autocar* and *Motor* magazines for permission to reproduce some of their road tests; Elvira Ruocco for archive pictures from Arese; Tim Holmes of Alfa GB for liaison and Ed McDonough for lists of scale models.

Thanks, too, to Mike Spenceley for the guided tour of Bertone coupé restoration and relevant photographs; Nicholas Froome of *Bolide News* for pictures from Goodwood testing, the Top Hat and GTA challenges; Julius Thurgood for background on the Top Hat series; Richard Everton, Willem van Voorthuyzen, Richard Drake and Jonathan Smith on competition preparation; Robert Petersson for the excellent photos of his GT Am and Sprint GT plus race preparation story; Giulietta Calabrese at Alfa Romeo GB for GTV picture and liaison; Nick Atkins for the Scuderia Monzeglio pic; Ulla-Carin Ekblom and Gunar Johansson for classic race shots; Ian Catt for archive photos; Goodwood and Silverstone circuits for the opportunity to photograph GTAs in action.

John Tipler

4

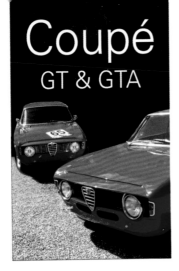

Contents

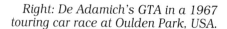

Coupé
GT & GTA

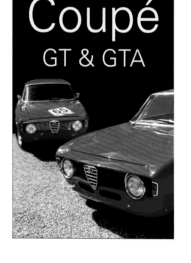

Right: De Adamich's GTA in a 1967 touring car race at Oulden Park, USA.

Far right: The race which provides his fondest memory, the 1966 6-Hours at Nürburgring which de Adamich won from pole position. He shared the car with Teodoro Zeccoli and, here, is ahead of Hubert Hahne's BMW1800ti.

Foreword by Andrea de Adamich

Andrea de Adamich.

I raced cars for 13 years of my life, from 1962 to 1974. Motor racing was my profession and it was a fabulous job being able to drive racing cars for a living. For many of those 13 years I was the official works Alfa Romeo driver, giving the new cars from Portello their racing debut following the company's long absence from the race tracks. Alfa Romeo's racing division was called Autodelta and it was run by Carlo Chiti.

I have fantastic memories, especially when I think of my name being linked to the debut of the GTA 1600 in 1965 and the debut of the TZ2 in the same year; then the introduction of the Tipo 33 2-litre in 1967, the 33-3 in 1969, together with the GTAm 2-litre, and lastly, for me at least, the 33-12 boxer in 1973.

The best memories, as far as excitement is concerned, are strangely enough linked to the GTA period. I was an up-and-coming driver then, with one foot in single-seaters, and the other in Touring and Grand Touring cars. Just think, my job at Autodelta enabled me to sponsor my exploits in Formula 3, and I actually won the Italian F3 Championship in 1965.

My experience in saloon car racing before the GTA appeared on the scene was with the Giulia TI Super Quadrifoglio, which was very fast at places like Monza, but a bit more difficult on complex circuits. It was a bit high, heavy in competition against the works Lotus Cortinas of John Whitmore and Trevor Taylor. I managed to win the 4-Hours at Monza in 1965 because the Grand Prix circuit and high-speed banked oval favoured me, but in other races it wasn't so easy.

I got my first run in a GTA at the Balocco test track and it was a revelation: so small, compact, low and light, and there was much potential to be developed. It was a car with everything to discover, both for the engineering team and for us drivers. As is often the case, the first races did not produce great results. First we were beaten in a hillclimb in Austria, which counted towards the European Championship. Then, although we were fastest in practice at Karlskoga, Sweden ahead of the Lotus Cortinas of Jackie Stewart and John Whitmore, when the race started I had a collision with Stewart at the first corner and had to retire. What bad luck!

Eventually the fine-tuning, development and testing began to bear fruit. During 1966 and 1967 the GTA was dominant all over Europe and I was European Touring Car Champion both years. What satisfaction it gave me to see those Lotus Cortinas finally in my rear-view mirror! To see the goatee-bearded Sir John Whitmore having difficulty maintaining my rhythm during practice and races was most rewarding!

I won everywhere with the GTA, by leaps and bounds, on tracks that were wet, dry, fast or slow, beating my competitors, who were often my team mates, as they had become my most serious rivals. There were many successes: the 4-Hours of Monza, 6-Hours at the Tourist Trophy at Oulton Park, the 500kms at Snetterton, the Zolder Cup, Budapest Grand Prix, and the Trophies at Zandvoort. Yet

the best memory I have is the timed practice for the 1966 6-Hours at the old Nürburgring, where the lap distance was 22kms. The battle was between Lotus Cortina, BMW and GTA. The fastest drivers were John Whitmore, Hubert Hahne and myself. Picture the scene; it's 4.00pm and we all practically finished the last practice lap together in a bid to set fastest lap for pole position for the big race the following day. The three of us are chatting together, waiting for the official times of the last lap to be announced over the loudspeaker. Electronic timekeeping like you have in Formula 1 today did not exist then, so you had to wait for the timekeepers to work out the times from their stop watches. Suddenly, the commentator announces, "GTA number 32, Andrea de Adamich ... 9 minutes 59.7 seconds." It's the first time a Touring car has lapped under 10 minutes, a new practice record! How exciting and what merry-making, even by my opponents, because at that time we weren't just competitors but friends also, and highly admired one another.

I could write a book about my career, but here I have to confine myself to the GTA period. And back then, I didn't just race on the track; I also had my street GTA to tool around in. It was replaced by the new 1750 GTV, which itself gave way to the 2000 GTV. Alfa Romeo's slogan in the 1950s was "The family car that wins races." It was also a slogan valid in my time between 1965-67, when the same cars as I drove on vacation, suitably prepared for

Opposite middle: Andrea de Adamich's motorsport career began in Alfa Romeo Giulia TI Supers, seen here at a checkpoint on the 1965 Rallye de Fiori.

competition, would win the European Touring Car Championships. I believe that the Alfa Romeo products of the time brought about a technological revolution in the world of average-displacement sports cars. And as so often happens with cars styled in Italy, it isn't just a matter of technical content, there is also the style content, in image and form, which is quite exclusive. I personally believe that the GTA, and the Bertone-styled GTs in general from that period, will always be regarded as

one of the very finest products from the House of Arese.

Still, a well-preserved GT from the late '60s has nothing to be ashamed of as far as form and performance are concerned when compared with cars designed and sold in recent years. The validity and competitive ability of the '65 GTA in classic car races goes to show that time passes, but the right technology is always victorious.

Andrea de Adamich

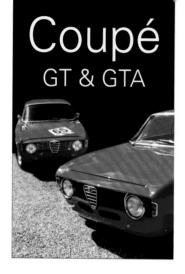

Coupé
GT & GTA

Introduction

The author's party at Snetterton for the 1968 500kms. Where are they now?

As a teenager in the mid-1960s I was part of a gang of motor racing enthusiast chums, male and female, who travelled to most of the British circuits at weekends to watch both club and international events. Often the journey was made in a borrowed parental Austin or Morris saloon, and on occasions of penury, one or two members of the gang would be transported the last few miles into the confines of the circuit in the boot of the car. Or perhaps entry would be obtained by crawling underneath some un-manned gate. I remember one such occasion was the British round of the European Touring Car Championship, an event we went to several years running at Norfolk's windswept Snetterton circuit, and this particular one was in 1966. This was the year Andrea de Adamich won in a GTA, of course, but actually a powerboat would have probably served him just as well, such were the conditions. Snetterton always seemed to suffer from extremes of climate.

Outright victory in these races, in the UK at any rate, was often the province of the V8-engined American monsters; Falcons, Galaxies or Mustangs, which rumbled their seemingly effortless way around. At the other end of the scale were the screaming hoards of Fiat-Abarth 1000s, which ran with Fiat 500 and 600 bodies, and whose boot-open stance caused not a little mirth, quickly turning to admiration as they crawled all over the Mini Coopers. There were the two-stroke Saab 93s, whose drivers seemed to take only a couple of seconds between each column gear change, and the occasional unwieldy

Mercedes limo, the rear wheels of which displayed simply outrageous angles of negative camber. For most of us though, it was the intense battles between the blood-red and gold Alan Mann Lotus Cortinas and the blood-red Alfa Romeo GTAs which were most enthralling. Sir John Whitmore was always a favourite, and we thought it hugely amusing that for several laps running he had time to wave to the photographers at the exit of Russell bend.

The BMW challenge was very much in its infancy, though the cars looked promising with their pop-rivetted wheelarch extensions; the occasional Porsche 911 would be in there, and it seemed odd at the time that it took a rally driver like Vic Elford to make them go properly. There was an exotic magic in the team names; Autodelta, Squadra Corse, Jolly Club, and the fact that our hero Jochen Rindt was in there driving an Alfa Romeo gave the proceedings added zest. One of my pals ran a Giulia 1300TI, and even went to the length of inscribing 'Autodelta SpA' on his overalls for when he serviced the car. 1966 was the first time I had seen the GTAs in action and it was a sight never to be forgotten. We gasped in awe as they came through the esses waggling their inside front wheels in the air, and were even more amazed when we saw they went all the way around Coram in a similar attitude.

In 1967 one of the Autodelta drivers was Rhoddy Harvey Bailey, and it was with some humour that when I interviewed him recently for *Performance Car* magazine, he drove me at indecent speed through the Peak

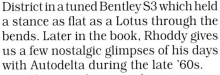

District in a tuned Bentley S3 which held a stance as flat as a Lotus through the bends. Later in the book, Rhoddy gives us a few nostalgic glimpses of his days with Autodelta during the late '60s.

The man who enjoyed most success with the GTA - at least in its earlier years - and who is regarded by Autodelta Director, Carlo Chiti, as the fastest of the GTA drivers, was Andrea de Adamich, and I was both flattered and delighted when he agreed to write the foreword for the book. Andrea is now a busy media figure in Italy, but in the Autodelta days he had some outstanding drives in Alfa Romeos of one sort or another. I was

in the JPS-Lotus pits at the Silverstone Grand Prix in 1973 when there was the almighty first lap shunt on the startline which virtually ended Andrea's racing career; I remember he was trapped for some time in his Brabham with a badly injured ankle.

Giorgetto Giugiaro styled the Giulia Coupé shape whilst working for Bertone, hence the tendency to use Bertone's name to identify the cars. Their styling is a timeless thing, always superbly proportioned, yet despite the fact that production of the shape lasted for more than a decade, they were never particularly commonplace outside of

Italy. This was possibly because they were always quite expensive cars to buy and, being fast and Italian, perceived as rather exotic and therefore difficult to maintain. Their successors, the Alfetta GTs, never won the heart in the same way as the Giulia Coupés although, again, there is little to criticise about the styling. As the 105-Series cars grew older, more fell by the wayside through neglect and owners being strapped for cash. Now it looks as if the classic car boom of the late 1980s has faded as a result of the international economic recession, and values of what is justifiably described as a 'classic' have failed to reach their potential; prices of original or restored Giulia Coupés took off too late in the wake of their supercar counterparts. This means they are still very much underrated and under-valued; but whether you are bothered or not by the investment potential of the cars, they will still provide more driving thrills and aesthetic pleasure than very many modern machines, as well as most of their contemporaries. During the last ten years a number of Alfa Romeo fans have raced them to good effect in club events and in particular the Owners' Club series, and some cars have looked more GTA than the real thing. Ford got it wrong for me with their slogan at the end of the '60s. The car I always promised myself was a GTA.

Sadly, since this book's original text was written, Malcolm Morris, Carlo Chiti and John Clifton have all passed away.

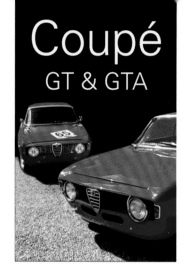

Coupé
GT & GTA

From Alfa
to Giulia

Alfa Romeo advertisment dating from 1919

Right: One of Alfa Romeo's early GT cars was the 6C 1750 produced between 1928 and 1933.

Alfa Romeo has been one of Italy's top three volume car producers since the early 1950s, along with Lancia and Fiat. The company was acquired in 1987 by Fiat, after a takeover battle with Ford, from the state-owned Finmeccanica group. The company joined Ferrari, Lancia, and the more recent arrival, Maserati, (51%) under the patriarchal Fiat penumbra. Although Alfa's history is full of attractive and soul-stirring coupés like the Bertone-styled Sprint GT derivatives of the 1960s which we are dealing with here, it is largely the charismatic and often idiosyncratic saloons which have earned its bread and butter from the early 1950s onwards, when the broad policy was to build a range of sports and grand touring cars alongside the saloons. However, the company's reputation still rests on its triumphs on the world's race circuits and gruelling endurance events, and it is a good idea to view the company's history as a whole before looking in detail at the coupés of the 1960s.

A.L.F.A.

Alfa Romeo was founded in 1910, making it Italy's second oldest sporting manufacturer, beaten by Itala by only two years. The company was originally set up in Naples as a subsidiary of the French Darracq concern in 1906 to sell off unwanted cars, but transferred to the labour-rich Milanese suburb of Portello the following year. Insufficient demand for the fragile and underpowered French cars broke the fledgling company, and it was re-formed as ALFA by Ugo Stella with Giuseppe

Merosi as chief designer. ALFA is an acronym for Anonima Lombarda Fabrica Automobili.

The first Alfas were very different from the pretty Darracqs; they were large and robust, with powerful engines and decent brakes, more appropriate for the poor state of the majority of Italian roads at the time. Merosi's first two cars were the 4.1-litre 24hp and the 2.4-litre 15hp. As far as their internals were concerned, these engines were a portent of the layout which Alfa has favoured throughout its history; twin overhead camshafts operating two rows of inclined valves, housed in hemispherical combustion chambers.

Also still retained today is what is essentially the original logo, which from the start comprised the familiar red cross of St George, (the arms of the city of Milan) combined with the medieval shield adornment of the Visconti family, a serpent devouring a child. The four-leaf-clover, or quadrifoglio motif which has nearly always featured on Alfa competition cars, appeared on engine and chassis number plates.

Nicola Romeo, Enzo Ferrari and Vittorio Jano

It didn't take long for Alfa to join in the competition fray, entering two 24hp cars for the arduous Sicilian road race, the Targa Florio of 1911, and although one car led the race, both eventually retired. Alfa's first taste of competition success came in 1913 when Campari and Franchini came third and fourth in the Coppa Florio. If the advent of the First World War prevented Merosi's promising 4-cylinder twin-cam Grand

6 C. GRAN TURISMO

Motore a 6 cilindri in linea e valvole in testa e doppio albero di distribuzione - Accelerazione fulminea - Guida gradevolissima, dolce e sicura - Perfetta stabilità e molleggio ottimo - Frenatura potentissima - Consumo per 100 Km. litri 13-14 di benzina - Velocità effettiva oltre i 115 Km.-ora. Potenza fiscale 21 HP.

Modelli di carrozzerie elegantissimi e confortevoli a 2 e 4 posti.

Prix car being raced, it also had the effect of introducing prosperous Milanese mining engineer, Nicola Romeo, to Alfa. By arrangement with Alfa's bankers, Romeo took over the Alfa plant in 1915 to produce compressors, tractors and Isotta aircraft engines for the war effort. When the war was over, Nicola Romeo became Managing Director and the company was henceforward called Alfa Romeo.

Two of the prewar cars were entered for the 1919 Targa Florio, running without success, but things improved from the early 1920s when the works Alfa Romeo team was run by one of the drivers, Enzo Ferrari. Race victories began with Campari's win at Mugello in 1920 and '21, and Sivocci

won the Targa Florio the following year driving Merosi's new 3-litre 6-cylinder type-RL. In 1924 Vittorio Jano's first design, the 2-litre supercharged straight-eight P2, won first time out at Cremona with Antonio Ascari at the wheel, and its first Grand Prix at Lyons driven by Campari. Although Ascari was killed in his P2 the following year at Montlhéry, the Alfa team had won sufficient races to gain them the first ever World Championship. This success was marked by the addition of a laurel wreath to the Alfa Romeo badge.

6C, 8C and P3:
beauty and performance

Whereas Merosi's road cars of the early '20s were conceptually much the same as his pre-war cars - robust, heavy and hardly sports cars - those of his successor Jano were different altogether, and much more closely related to the racing cars. The engines were shorn of superchargers and two of their cylinders but, at first, were given only a set of vertical valves and a single camshaft. Open-top lightweight bodies on race-developed chassis completed the transformation. These were the 6C 1500 and 6C 1750 of 1927, soon superseded by twin-cam Super Sport and 100mph Gransport versions with superchargers. Alfa

Romeo's, and arguably the world's, first grand touring car came next in the saloon-bodied version known as the 1750 Gran Turismo.

Enzo Ferrari had set up his racing headquarters at Modena in 1929 to run the works Alfas and maintain customers' competition cars, and in the early 1930s Alfa Romeo virtually dominated international competition. The car which accomplished so much was Jano's 2.3-litre straight-eight 8C 2300, winning Le Mans in four consecutive years from 1931 to 1935. The Grand Prix version of the 8C won its first race, the 1931 European Grand Prix at Monza, and it was known as

the Monza from then onwards. What was remarkable about the design of this engine was that it was basically two four-cylinder twin-cam engines facing each other with the camshaft drive in the centre. The advantage of this curious layout was that it allowed for shorter cams and cranks and was therefore more reliable in theory; there were also manufacturing advantages. This proved to be the case, for when fitted to the P3 grand prix car it clocked up at least 40 major successes between 1932 and 1935, most notable of which was probably Nuvolari's victory at the Nürburgring in 1935 against the mighty German 'silver arrows'.

Bimotore: the original "il Mostro"?

By way of counter-attacking the Mercedes and Auto Unions, Scuderia Ferrari introduced the fearsome twin-engined Bimotore in 1935, which used two P3 engines, one behind and one in front of the driver, who sat on top of a three-speed gearbox which drove the rear wheels. The car was capable of 200mph in a straight line, but a ravenous appetite for tyres marked it as a failure.

Meanwhile, things were not going well for the company financially. Ownership passed from the Banco di Sconto into government receivership and

Unbeatable for styling panache? The 1937 8C 2900B by Touring.

Alfa Romeo was refloated with its sights set on more diverse commercial markets, including trucks, coaches, marine and aircraft engines. Cars for the domestic market took the form of handsome, but hardly outstanding, four-door saloons, powered by straight-six engines of 1900cc or 2300cc. The 6C 2300's box-section chassis was considerably lighter than the C-section girders of its 8C 2300 predecessor, and its sales performance was sufficient to keep the factory going as a commercial proposition.

Short-wheelbase sports chassis were offered with bodies by Zagato, Castagna, Farina and Touring. Three coupé versions with Touring coachwork took the first three places in a 24-hour race at Pescara, and one came fourth in the 1937 Mille Miglia. Alfa successes in this fabulous event were legion: with the exception of 1931, one type of Alfa or another won it outright from 1928 to 1938. Most notable were the 8C 2900As, which took the first three places in 1936.

By the end of the decade, though, production vehicles were leaving the factory in a trickle. Under Mussolini's direction, the main thrust was to be seen to match the German cars on the Grand Prix circuit. Jano's last creation in 1937, before leaving under a cloud for Lancia and later Ferrari, was the twin-supercharged V12. It produced some 430bhp, which was more than the rear differential could cope with, and in the wake of this failure, Alfa lost the services of the man who had been perhaps their greatest asset. Other engine designs were pressed into service, including the 3-litre V16 which managed second place in the 1938 Italian Grand Prix. The wide-angle V12 engine was tried in the Tipo 162, and a mid-mounted flat-twelve in the all-independent suspension Tipo 512 but, unfortunately, development of this highly promising car was stalled by the advent of the Second World War.

Before hostilities began, Germanic victories on the Grand Prix circuit had become so predictable that the promoters introduced voiturette racing as an entertaining diversion. This class was hotly contested but, nevertheless, proved to be the salvation of Alfa Romeo's morale, as the company managed to find success with the Gioacchino Columbo-designed single-supercharger straight-eight Tipo 158 Alfettas.

Farina, Fangio and the fabulous 159

Nicola Romeo died on 15th August 1938, and therefore missed the devastation of the Portello factory. Its 8500 workforce had been involved in the Italian war effort, and as a consequence it was a natural target for Allied bombing raids. The factory was hit twice in 1943 and again in 1944. Despite this major setback, production of aero and marine engines was maintained, and the racing programme resumed almost the moment hostilities had ceased. The car which was used was the pre-war 1.5-litre Tipo 158, and with its derivative, the 159, Alfa Romeo achieved complete supremacy in the postwar years, right up to 1951. There were 25 Grand Prix victories in the hands of, among others, Giuseppe Farina and Juan Manuel Fangio, who won the first two World Championships in 1950 and 1951.

When the formula changed, and in the face of increasing success by Ferrari, Alfa Romeo withdrew from Formula 1, not returning to that particular arena until 1970 when they provided V8 engines for the up-and-coming McLaren and March teams.

If the 1980s represented something of a nadir in Alfa Romeo's sporting heritage, its credibility as a maker of production models was simultaneously tarnished by the rust crisis, which also hit Lancia and Fiat, and to be fair not many of the European manufacturers escaped entirely. The rot set in, as it were, during the 1970s, a legacy of

importing and using adulterated 'Iron Curtain' steel. Possibly what carried the company through these troubled times was the enduring support of a core of enthusiasts who continued to buy and use Alfa products.

Alfa Romeo's participation in motorsport has been somewhat episodic. It has seemed to ebb and flow with waves of corporate enthusiasm, but in sports car racing things never seemed quite so gloomy as in the Formula 1 debacles of the '70s and '80s, although Alfa Romeo has always lacked the consistency, commitment and even the administrational aptitude of Ferrari. After the company's withdrawal from works involvement in competition in 1953, many private owners went racing in events like the Mille Miglia, Giro D'Italia and the Carrera Messicana, with

The Giulietta SZ 1300 carried the torch for Alfa Romeo in competition during the late 1950s and early 1960s.

Centre: Not a straight line to be seen: the curvaceous Giulietta SS was built between 1957 and 1962.

Below: 750-Series Giulietta Sprint, styled by Bertone, and in production from 1954-1962.

their production-based 1900 saloons, Giulietta Sprints and SSs, Zagato-bodied SZ coupés, and Pininfarina Spiders, and there were very many successes at this level.

Back to the races! Autodelta

The Alfa management got serious about racing again in 1964 and bought Carlo Chiti's Autodelta Racing Team, which formed the basis for virtually all works competition activity until 1985. Most of Autodelta's victories were achieved in the mid-to-late '60s with the Giulia TZ (TZ 1) coupés in grand touring car racing, and GTA coupés in production car events. The car which contested the sports-prototype category was the fragile Tipo 33, first raced in 1967 with almost no success whatsoever. It was a pity that Autodelta had abandoned the TZ 2 and GTA projects to concentrate on the sports-prototype category.

The mid-engined 2-litre V8 held considerable potential, however, and Tipo 33-2s finished well up in events like the BOAC 500kms at Brands Hatch, the Targa Florio, and Le Mans in 1968. Not until 1971 did reliability and performance improve sufficiently for the 3-litre V8-engined 33-3 to notch up some meaningful successes, including victories in the BOAC race and the Targa Florio. With sports car racing dominated by Ferrari and then Matra over the following two seasons, Autodelta had to be content with just a handful of placings. With very little works opposition, the flat-12 engined

In 1962 production moved to the all-new factory at Arese in north-west Milan; here, late 1960s 1750 GTVs go down the line.

Below left: The range of Alfa models posed in the Edgware Road workshop of Alfa GB circa 1966: Giulia TI, Duetto, Sprint GT and 1300 TI.

33/TT 12 had more or less everything its own way in 1975, and again in 1977, but without top class competition the World Championship victories were rather hollow ones.

Bertone creates the Giulia 105 coupé

Meanwhile, production carried on apace with the Giulia 105-Series saloons replacing the 101-Series Giuliettas as bread-and-butter models in 1962, and our subject, the Giulia Sprint GT and its derivatives, were first shown at Frankfurt in 1963. Later the 105-Series Pininfarina Spider launched in 1966 epitomised sports car motoring for a newly-wealthy generation. By 1963 production facilities had moved from Portello, which was restricted from further development by a housing estate, to a new factory complex at Arese on the outskirts of Milan. The company's Balocco test track near Turin was opened the following year in 1964.

By 1969, annual production had reached 100,000 units. The staider-looking 1750 and 2000cc Berlinas supplemented the fluted and scalloped Giulia saloons in 1967 and the range was augmented yet again when the Alfettas were introduced in 1972. There was considerable overlap of production, as the last Giulia Nuovas were built in 1977.

1750 Berlinas outside Alfa GB's Edgware Road showrooms in 1969.

Below: The glassfibre-bodied spaceframe chassis Giulia TZ2 in the pits at Vallelunga in 1967; Carlo Chiti directs operations.

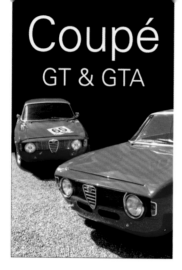

Coupé
GT & GTA

2

**Bertone's
105 Coupé.
From
Drawing Board
to the
World's
Showrooms**

As a young man during the '30s, Nuccio Bertone used to have an annual tour selling his father's car styling exercises, and after the war his own career as a stylist started to take off when he sold a pair of MG chassis clothed with bodies of his own design to US entrepreneur Wacky Arnolt.

The original Batmobiles
Alfa Romeo management was impressed with these cars, and commissioned Bertone, who was at the time mostly a weekend racer and aerodynamic theorist, to draw a successor to the Touring-styled Disco Volante. What Bertone gave them was the series of extraordinary Berlina Aerodinamica Technica, or 'BAT', cars. The original car was based on the regular 1900 Super Sprint, itself a popular car for 'reworking' by the top carrozzerie,

including Touring, Ghia, Castagna, Boano, and Zagato. These exercises in classical coupé coachwork styling can also be seen as heralds of the Giulia Sprint GT but, in spirit, the 2600 Sprint is closer.

Bertone's other contribution to Alfa Romeo's search for a satisfactory replacement for the Disco Volante project was the beautifully elegant 2000 Sportiva of 1954. Based on a 1900 Super chassis, the Sportiva also had a De Dion rear suspension set-up, and there are elements of the Sportiva's design, particularly the rear-end treatment, which can be detected in the subsequent Giulietta and Giulia Sprints.

Win a Sprint!
Alfa Romeo were planning the introduction of the Giulietta range

Right: Giugiaro's first job at Bertone Studios was to style the 2000 Sprint Coupé built between 1960 and 1962. This is a 2600 Sprint Coupé, in production from 1962 to 1966.

Opposite bottom: Profile of the fabulous and stylistically advanced 1954 2000 Sportiva.

Below: The 101-Series Giulietta Sprint of 1960 with the revised grille, side indicators and badges.

in 1953, and they incorporated the drawings of Bertone and his chief designer Franco Scaglione to produce the design for the Sprint. This model would be the first to use Orazio Satta Puliga's brand new all-alloy twin-cam engine, the one still available today in the Alfa 75, 155 and 164. The story of how Bertone produced a car for the Turin Show with but 20 days to spare, and the fact that Alfa Romeo financed its development by running a lottery with the prizes being no less than 500 brand new Sprints, is legendary. The Italian media had hyped the lottery, and enthusiasm for the prospect of an affordable sporting Alfa coupé was nearing fever pitch. As the date for the drawing of the lottery came and went, the ticket holders grew furious,

and it was with some corporate relief that Bertone produced the Turin Show car as a demonstration of Alfa's good intentions. Bertone was asked to make the prize-winners' cars, and by degrees he went on to make about 6000 Sprints. Total Sprint production was 29,042 units, including Veloce and 1300 models.

The success of the Giulietta Sprint catapulted Bertone into the big time, and he had to move to a new plant to cope with demand. Over the years, Bertone employed a number of extremely talented stylists, such as Giorgetto Giugiaro and Marcello Gandini, and this has led to disputes over attributions; the Lamborghini Miura is the most famous instance, with all three men named by various sources as the designer. The truth is probably that there was input from all three, with Bertone, as principal, having the final say. In any event, although Giugiaro styled the 105-Series Giulia Sprint GT while he was with Bertone, it is the firm itself which gets the credit, as it does for all Alfa Romeo's production coupés built during the Giulietta-Giulia era, with Zagato cladding the 750- and 101-Series racing coupés and later Junior Zs, and Pininfarina is the toast of Spider owners. The equally well conceived Berlinas are Bertone designs, with firms like Colli producing the Giardinetta and Promiscua estate bodies. Another show car designed by Bertone was the Canguro of 1964 which used 105-Series running gear in a sophisticated spaceframe chassis. It had a sleek GT body comparable with the TZ1.

The Giulietta and Giulia Sprints and their derivatives are the forerunners of the 105-Series Giulia Sprint GTs. The cars may look straightforward enough, but sorting out the serial numbers is a complicated affair, for there are seemingly illogical overlaps in specifications, names and numbers. Broadly, it boils down to the 750- and 101- designations, which refer to type numbers, although 750-Series Sprints, confusingly, have chassis numbers beginning 1493; "750" was the factory number originally applied to the front-wheel-drive mini-Berlina project, which never progressed beyond the prototype. More logically, 101-Series Sprint chassis numbers start 10102.3. The Sprint Speciale and Sprint Zagato were only built as 101-Series cars. 750-Series bodies were made up to April 1958, 750-Series engines until September 1959; 101-Series bodies were produced from April 1958, and 101-Series engines came in from September 1959. The actual model, the Giulietta Sprint, was in production from 1955 to 1962, with a slight facelift in 1959. In 1962 the engine was bored and stroked from 1300 (1290cc) to 1600 (1570cc), becoming the 101-Series Giulia Sprint, (chassis numbers start 10112.3 ...) with both engine options and five-speed gearbox, which remained in production until 1964. Each and every engine was stripped and checked after being run on the test bed before being installed in the cars. Unimaginable for today's manufacturers!

Within these numerical divisions came the Veloce (or 'swift') versions, which ushered in, in 1956, a major

reworking of the 1300 twin-cam and twin Weber carburettors, which took power up from 65 to 90bhp. A floor-mounted gearchange rowed it along. We tend to regard drum brakes as being old-fashioned nowadays, but those used by the Giuliettas were excellent and certainly well respected in their day. The Giulietta Sprint Veloce with its perspex windows, was fast, agile, and a match for many larger-engined '50s grand touring cars. The Veloce model was introduced again as a 112bhp version of the Giulia 101-Series Spider (the Sprint Speciale also got the Veloce engine in 1963). All models were equipped with Dunlop disc brakes at this point, but these were regarded as a poor substitute for the exotic, finned drums which, on the Giulias, had three leading shoes 2.75 inches wide at the front!

Although visually alike, if not quite identical, the 750-Series bodies were more 'hand-made' and there was more seam-welding; on the other hand, the 101-Series bodies made more use of pressings, with panels spot-welded. Externally, the most obvious difference between 750- and 101-Series Giulietta and Giulia Sprints is the treatment of front grille (originally the property of the Romeo van) and the grilles each side of it. On the later car, they are bolder than the delicate ones of the 750 Giulietta Sprint, and the later model's front wings are cluttered with "1300" or "1600" and "Bertone" badges, as well as side indicators on European-spec cars. Tail lights, too, are more prominent. The Sprint escaped the fake air-intake on the bonnet of the 101-Series Spider, the real purpose of which was to gain

sufficient height to accommodate the taller block of the 1600 engine in the smaller engine bay of the Spider.

Contemporary with the 101-Series Coupés were the 2000 four- and 2600 Sprint straight-six Coupés, Giugiaro's first piece of work during his time at Bertone Studios. They were the siblings of the Touring-styled 2000 and 2600 Spiders. "Sprint" seemed a singularly inappropriate title for this model, for it was larger, more costly, and belonged in the realms of traditional grand touring cars, like the Gordon-Keeble, which was another contemporary Bertone exercise. The 2600 Sprint had a similar line to Giugiaro's next opus, the Giulia 'Bertone' coupé, and could easily be regarded as its big sister.

Giulia Ti, the first 105

The name "Giulia" implies a grown-up "Giulietta", and in effect this was the case with the 105-Series cars. Use of the rather obvious Giulietta name is said to have originated at the launch of the Alfa 1900-Series in 1950, when a Russian prince remarked of the factory engineers and drivers that there were many Romeos present, but no Giulietta. Someone at the factory picked up on this, and the appellation was given to the 750-Series Sprint coupé which was introduced in 1954.

The first of the 105-Series cars was built in 1962 at the all-new Arese plant north-west of Milan. It was the 5-speed, column-change Giulia TI saloon, a remarkably efficient design for all its much maligned stumpiness. The cd figure of 0.33 was the lowest of all the 105-Series models, (the Sprint-GT had

a cd of 0.37), and in fact beats much of what's around today. It was achieved by giving the design the steeply sloping windscreen - just take a look at the curvature at the corners which allows such a rake - and the lip at the trailing edge of the roof. The rear panel was also truncated in a deliberate attempt to copy the Kammtail of the long-tailed Giulietta SZ of 1959; the aerodynamic theories of Professor Wunibald Kamm had for some time been adhered to by racing sports car manufacturers, and the square-tail SZ exemplifies this.

Other styling quirks which make the Giulia TI and later Super shape so charming are the flutes which run along the top of the car's wings, from front to back, which are echoed by similar scallops along the edge of the roof. There were distinct similarities between the front suspension componentry of the TI and the TZ1 (or GTZ if you prefer), and it is hard to know which begat what. At any rate, the factory competition variant was known as the TI Super, which came out in 1963 and was built with slightly thinner-gauge panels than the regular TI, and the rear doors were fitted with perspex windows. There was no sound insulation, bucket type seats were screwed to the floor and it got Campagnolo alloy wheels. Armed with the TZ1 and Giulia SS specification engine and floor shift, it was hugely successful in all kinds of events all over the world during the early '60s.

Giulia Sprint GT, Bertone's 105 Coupé

The 105-Series Giulia Sprint GT was announced in 1963, and was

immediately acclaimed as a suitable successor to the 101-Series cars. The engine was the 1570cc unit with five-speed gearbox, and there were servo assisted Dunlop disc brakes all round. Most electrics were now Bosch and Marelli, which were considered to be a huge improvement over the Lucas equipment used previously. The water-cooled engine was all-aluminium, with cast iron cylinder liners and had hemispherical combustion chambers with the spark plugs in the top. The valves opened and closed by means of inverted-bucket tappets, operated by chain-driven camshafts. Exhaust valves were sodium-cooled and the crankshaft had five main bearings. Power output was quoted as 122bhp gross, 106bhp net, at 6000rpm, giving a top speed of 113mph and a 0-60mph acceleration time of 11.3 seconds. In practice, figures quicker than these were easily achievable. Front suspension was independent by double wishbones, coil springs and dampers, with an anti-roll bar. The rear suspension consisted of a live axle, on coil springs and dampers, located by lower trailing arms and a reaction trunnion. The Giulia Sprint GT ran on 155 x 15 Pirelli Cinturato tyres. *Road & Track* magazine praised the willingness of the engine and the Sprint GT's ability to cover ground quickly, delighting in the five-speed box, shifting at 6500rpm for maximum performance. Personally, that's not something I do very often with an Alfa engine, and you certainly don't need to with the torquier 2-litre engines. On second thoughts, maybe the GTV6 on a race track is a different matter ...

As if the car wasn't stylish enough, Alfa's model adds a touch of glamour to the GTA of 1965.

The Sprint GT's instrument layout included an 8000rpm tachometer and 140mph speedometer placed right in front of the driver, with auxiliary instruments, fuel, oil pressure, oil and water temperature in two similarly sized dials each side of the main gauges. All 105-Series saloons and coupés had the quirky but nonetheless endearing windscreen wiper movement which can be likened to folded arms when stationary, but choreographed to just miss each other when in operation, the one blade closing over the other. There were single speed wipers on early cars (including the Sprint GT), graduating to two speeds, which on a Giulia 1300 TI I owned, amounted to slow and regular, but they got the job done reasonably efficiently though.

The GTC: "C" for convertible

The Sprint GT was joined in 1965 by three more 105-Series cars; one was the competition derivative, the Sprint GTA, which is described fully in the racing chapter; the second was the Giulia Super saloon and the third was the Giulia GTC.

The GTC was, in effect, a Sprint GT with the top cut off and the shell extensively stiffened and braced in the floor and around both front and rear bulkheads. The exercise was carried out by Touring of Milan, which was fast going down the tubes at the time and soon to become part of Alfa Romeo; half

Bertone, half Touring, the GTC was undoubtedly one of the most stylish cabriolets ever made. Production lasted from 1964 to 1966, during which time a mere thousand were built.

The Giulia Super on the other hand remained in production for a whole decade, terminating with the Nuova Super, its bonnet and boot smoothed out; the quintessential Super remains one of my favourite Alfas. Identical to the TI apart from upgraded trim details, floor shift and changed differential ratios, plus twin Webers instead of a single Solex, the Giulia Super was based on the same floorpan with a longer wheelbase, and was mechanically almost identical to the Giulia Sprint GT. In 1965, the Giulia Super cost £1547, and the lower specification TI, which stood for Turismo Internationale, was

Top left: The rare GTC; this is Tim Spitzel's car in a Club sprint at Duxford.

Centre left: Probably better than new, Richard Banks' GTC basks in sunshine.

Below: A trio of Giulias visiting the Italian Lakes: a GT 1300 Junior, a 1300 Giulia TI and a Giulia Super. The steeply raked windscreen and cut-off tail gave the Giulia TI a cd of just 0.33.

Top right: A GT 1300 Junior. The model was in production from 1966 to 1971; the bonnet is flush with the front panel on this car so it must be post-1971. With Alfas, there is always a degree of overlap, however.

Below: Giulia saloon and coupé bodyshells side-by-side on the production lines at Arese.

£150 cheaper. By comparison, the GTC at £1937 was top of the range, since the Sprint GT cost £1849. As we shall see, the GTA was in a league of its own, being nearly £1000 more expensive still.

GTV: "V" for Veloce, a faster car?

There have been Veloce high-performance options throughout the various model ranges, from the Giulietta Sprint Veloce which boasted nearly 40 per cent more power than its sister, through the various GTVs which, in the Alfetta era, referred merely to the 2-litre coupé, to the Alfa 75 Veloce which benefits, if only

Centre: In 1967 the 1600 engine was stretched to 1779cc and the cars called 1750 GTVs. This model became known retrospectively as the "Mark 1". Front sidelights mounted on the bumper identify the model.

Bottom: The Mark 2 1750 GTV of 1970 has the sidelights in the front panel and overriders on the bumper. There are now side indicators and trim changes, plus piston mods and dual-circuit brakes.

in the aesthetics department, from a factory body-kit. The difference between the 750/101-Series cars and the 105-Series Coupés was that Veloce actually *meant* something in the earlier cars, like an extra carburettor or lightweight panels, whereas it signified rather less in the later models. The Veloce version of the Sprint GT, the 1600 Sprint GT Veloce, was introduced in 1966, and offered improved performance by virtue of its smaller inlet ports; they were down to 30mm from 33mm, and the car felt a lot stronger and eager with just this small modification. Quoted increase was a mere 3bhp, but torque was substantially better, and at lower revs; Paddy McNally writing in *Autosport* in 1967, said the "modifications make the Veloce a much better car." Although valve lift was increased and cam timing was revised, the cams themselves were the same as the regular Sprint GT. Tyres were Cinturato SRs on narrow 4 1/2J rims, and the brakes were servo-assisted ATE. Despite different seats the Veloce interior was much the same as the Sprint GT which, today, would be described as utilitarian, although it was not unsophisticated in 1966.

GT 1300 Junior: return of the Giulietta?

The Giulia Sprint GT 1300 Junior was around from 1966 to 1977, and during this time won many friends for Alfa Romeo amongst the world's motoring press, who had cars on long-term loan. As an entry-level model, its advantage in Italy was one of lower taxation. Australia's *Motor Manual* saw it as a reincarnated Giulietta, acknowledging

that its 1290cc engine and five-speed box "requires a little skill to use its abilities to the full. Unless the right gear is used at the right time, performance is downright mediocre. But scrambling up and down the five synchromeshed ratios is enjoyable." The GT 1300 Junior also got the 1600's camshafts, twin carbs and the reduced port sizes which so benefited the 1600 GT Veloce; in fact the GT 1300 Junior had almost as much torque as the old Sprint GT. In 1969, *Autocar* had the top speed of this 90bhp car at a true 100mph, with 106mph indicated. 0-60mph was achieved in 12.6 seconds, but on the move on a twisty road the GT 1300 Junior was reckoned to be great fun. In 1969, it would cost you £1749, against a Lancia Fulvia 1.3 at £1698. In 1971, the GT 1300 Junior was facelifted using 1750 parts and trim, with revised front end styling. In 1972 the model range was extended when the 1600 engine was used again for the GT coupé. These two, the GT 1300 Junior and GT Junior 1.6, got the 2000 GTV bodyshell from 1974, with differing rear lights, and were available right to the end of 105-Series production in 1977.

1750: back to the thirties

In order to increase performance in the late 1960s, Alfa Romeo took the straightforward route of enlarging engine capacity, just as Porsche went on to do with the 911 engine, and all four variants of the Alfa twin-cam, from 1300cc to 2-litres, have found their way at some time into the entire range of 105-Series coupés and Spiders. Giulia saloons used 1300cc

and 1600cc engines, as did the Junior Zagato coupés, whereas the Berlinas got 1750cc and 2000cc units.

Thus the successor to the Giulia Sprint GT Veloce was the 1750 GT Veloce, in which the engine was bored out to 80mm, which in practice involved fitting bigger piston liners and a longer stroke (88.5mm) nitrided crankshaft. Cubic capacity was now 1779cc, but for marketing purposes it was convenient to describe the cars as 1750s, harking back to the successful 1750s of the '30s. The front panel now became flush with the bonnet and wings, so the tiny gap previously visible under the leading edge of the Sprint GT bonnet disappeared. Other stylistic differences include twin headlights set in a matt black grille, and in what became known retrospectively as the "Mark 1" 1750, the front sidelight/indicator units were incorporated into the outer reaches of the bumper, and in the later 1970 Mark 2 version, the bumpers differed and sprouted overriders and the sidelight clusters were located in the front panel beneath the headlights.

From 1968 the 1750 GTV used wider, 5.5 inch, 14 inch diameter wheels, instead of the Sprint GT's 4.5 inch, 15 inch diameter wheels, and the wheelarch shape altered. There were bigger brakes, too, and a revised air filter but, apart from a slightly taller engine block, which you wouldn't notice, the 1750's only other distinguishing feature was its rear anti-roll bar. A hydraulically operated diaphragm clutch was introduced replacing the cable operated clutch of previous models. The 1750 GTV's wheelbase

Opposite left, top to bottom -

1. Mark 1 1750 GTV has sidelight mounted on front bumper.

2. Mark 2 1750 GTV has sidelight in front panel and bumper overrider.

3. This type of rear light only used on the Mark 1 1750 GTV.

4. Mark 2 1750 reverted to original style rear light cluster.

5. 2000 GTV rear light cluster includes a reversing lamp. All other models had a central reversing light under the bumper.

Below: Access to shapely rear seats of the GT 1300 Junior, cramped for adults but excellent for children.

was 92.5 inches, 3.9 inches longer than the Spider's which would suggest, with the lengthy overhangs front and rear, that the Spider's handling would be far inferior to the coupé's. In fact, this is not necessarily true, because the Spider has good weight distribution, but can be very tail-happy in the wet.

The 1750 GTV got a mildly dished wood-rimmed wheel with the horn buttons located in the three spokes, and wood veneer and vinyl was much in evidence elsewhere in the trim department. The siting of the instruments was first class, with speedo and rev-counter in twin binnacles sitting proud of the fascia, whilst the auxiliary dials were angled towards the driver in the central console above the gear lever. The oil pressure gauge was built into the rev counter. Switches for fan, wipers and instrument lights were below the lever, as the console curved down between the seats. Indicators, side and headlights and dip controls were on stalks to the left of the steering column. The seats were rather more sports orientated than the Sprint GT's, and those of the Mk 2 were sufficiently supportive to win top marks from two orthopaedic surgeons in a survey.

1750 GTV or Jaguar E-type?

When new in 1968, the 1750 GTV cost £2248 in the UK, compared with its rivals, which included the Elan Plus 2 at £2119, the BMW 2002 at £1597, Porsche 912 at a surprisingly high £2783. A 2+2 E-type Jaguar was priced around £2300, and was rather more powerful, whilst a Lotus Cortina cost a mere £1162, and a Fiat 124 Coupé was £1438. If money was not the principal object, GTV alternatives might have been a choice between the Porsche 911 and the Lancia Flavia 1800/2000.

Writing about the 1750 GTV in *MotorSport* in 1968, Andrew Marriott pointed out that "When cars cost £2250, they have to be something special, for such a sum would pay halfway towards a fairly decently-sized house outside the Home Counties."

When testing the car in 1968, *Motor* magazine described the characteristics as "... unchanged in essentials. There is less roll than in earlier cars, but the Michelin XAS tyres squealed rather easily. The curious Alfa lurching movements when near the limit have

Insignia on C-post started off on Sprint GT Veloce as green cloverleaf on ivory circle and changed to gold on white with the 1750 GTV.

Below: Most obvious external change to the Bertone Coupé in its 2000 GTV configuration is the all-alloy design of the grille and shield. Rear lights are bigger, trim is in cloth.

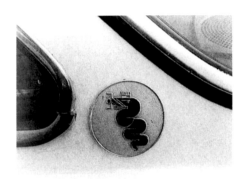

Milanese symbol and Alfa logo of serpent devouring child forms insignia on 2000 GTV C-post.

also been diminished. When trying really hard, such as on a circuit, the inside wheel will lift and spin at speeds up to 70mph, producing a mildly disconcerting oversteer." John Bolster writing in *Autosport* in 1969 said the 1750 was "... the kind of car that even an experienced test driver will take out for the sheer fun of handling it." The 1750 GTV was higher geared than the 1600 GTV, so its acceleration was not that much faster, but the general reduction in effort and improvement in refinement at cruising speeds made the 1750 a great deal more sophisticated.

"Iniezione" for the USA
Although the 1750 GTV appeared in Europe in January 1968, it did not become available in the US until 1969. The US-spec cars got Spica mechanical fuel injection, unpopular these days, and an "iniezione" badge on the boot. They were the basis for the GTAm competition cars, of which more in the racing chapter. The 1750 GTV was available until 1971, and alongside it was marketed the GT 1300 Junior. The Mark 1 1750, produced until 1970, was notable for its rough-sounding engine, which was the consequence of high-compression piston slap. Mark 2 pistons with offset gudgeon-pins, together with improved camshafts, were used to alleviate this symptom, and a second brake servo for dual-circuit brakes was added on right-hand-drive cars. Alfa devotees rate the 1750 GTV as the nicest of the Bertone Coupés and, as my first Alfa was a 1750 Berlina, I can readily testify to the delightful willingness of that particular engine; there is a school of

thought which believes the stiffer Berlina and Super chassis to provide superior handling characteristics to the coupés, and indeed the Spiders. This is based on the relationship of the unsprung weight of the axle to the mass of the rear of the car. In a practical sense, the saloons may be a better bet than the coupés, but when it comes to aesthetics, the coupé styling is in a class of its own.

2-litres and limited slip
In 1971 came the capacity increase which created the torquier 2-litre engine, achieved by enlarging the bore size from 80mm to 84mm (although the 1750 was still available through the 1971 model year). European cars could be delivered with twin Webers, Dell'Ortos, or even Solex carburettors. Enthusiasts claim the first two makes are the best. With their increased torque, the 2-litre cars could pull more efficiently at low revs, ultimately developing around 130bhp at 5500rpm.

The increase in capacity was achieved by increasing the bore size, but since head gasket sealing had been marginal even with the 1750 engines, Alfa engineers shifted the bore centres and machined the block so there was more metal between the liners. The head was worked differently as well and accommodated bigger valves. 2-litre cars also benefited from the fitting of a limited slip differential, optional at first but standard on UK imports from 1972, which put paid to inside-rear wheelspin and enabled them to get more traction out of a slow or slippery bend, and balancing the handling better, too. The cars got bigger brakes as well.

Visually, the 2-litre coupé differs most obviously from the 1750 in the treatment of its radiator grille. In the later vehicle there is no separate stainless steel Alfa shield shape; instead it is formed from slatted strips of zinc alloy, with the shield shape standing just proud of the rest of the grille. Frankly, they should have left it how it was. Apart from the "2000" badge on the back panel, the rear light clusters are significantly larger and incorporate reversing lights. Interiors are much revised, with seats now in cloth trim if required, and the dash itself has less of the purist sporting appeal of the 1750 GTV. The instruments have more prominent hoods, perspex instead of glass lenses, and the auxiliaries move up between the two big dials.

Like late Juniors and Spiders in UK and Europe, 2000 GTVs were known as 115-Series cars in the 'States, due to chassis numbering, and they were only available there from 1972 to 1974. Like the US-spec 1750 GTV, they ran with Spica injection, which was the product of Alfa Romeo's Spica division. The pump had already been used for diesel engines, and it did service in cars as disparate as the Montreal, GTAm, and turbocharged F1 cars. In retrospect, the injection system was not a great success and, unless properly maintained by Alfa experts, could be problematic. This has resulted in cars with dud injection being sold cheaply in the 'States to European speculators. Perhaps it should be mentioned that the Bosch L Jetronic, which replaced the Spica system in 1982 and was

Right: Interiors of the three main evolutions of the Giulia Coupé: Giulia Sprint GT has austere interior with flat bakelite wheel.

Below right: The 1750 GTV gets more sophisticated dash and wood trim wheel.

used in the 2000 Spider and GTV6, was a huge improvement in terms of response and accuracy.

Road wheel styles changed to alloy for the late model GTV 2000 SE, which was a UK-only, end-of-line clearance, but this had more to do with relieving the cars of their rusty steel wheels, for they had stood around in the open for too long. For the same reason they were also given the dubious luxury of a vinyl-covered roof, because it was a cheaper expedient than a respray. Not only was this unpleasant aesthetically but when the covering became unglued, moisture trapped underneath set about its corrosive process. SEs also had tinted glass, a black grille, rubbing strips and a radio cassette player. The original 105-Series steel wheels with the characteristic air holes running around the outside of the hub had chrome hubcaps on the Sprint GT and 1750 GTV, losing the chrome hubcaps with the 2000 GTV when another type of wheel trim was applied and, inevitably, other aftermarket alloys were sometimes fitted.

Another little detail which changed along the way was the cloverleaf emblem on the C-pillar. It started off as a green cloverleaf on an ivory circle for the Giulia Sprint 1600 GTV, going to gold on white for the 1750 GTV, and finally ended up cast in metal with the serpent

Left: The 2000 GTV has auxilliary instruments in binnacle and cloth seat trim. The woodrim wheel is now very dished.

Below left: The GTC shares the Sprint GT's austere fascia.

and child in green for the 2000 GTV. From 1972, the word "Milano" was dropped from the Alfa Romeo badge, in deference to the opening of the Alfasud factory at Pomigliano d'Arco. Bertone badges feature throughout on the front wings.

Production of new and old Alfa models has always overlapped, the outgoing model on the next line to the newcomer, and so it was with the 105-Series Coupés, which were still trickling off the lines as late as 1977. Alongside were the 116-Series Alfetta GTs, also conceptually Giugiaro designs, but which, with their aluminium-cased transaxle gearboxes, inboard rear brakes, De Dion rear suspension and torsion bar front end, were different characters altogether.

Montreal: 105-Series Supercar

Other 105-Series derivative coupés which should be mentioned are the Bertone-styled Montreal, a two-seater coupé which, despite its 2.6-litre four-cam V8 engine from the sports-racing Tipo 33 (with reduced bore sizes), was based on the Giulia Sprint GT floorpan. When it was first shown at the Montreal World Trade Fair in 1967, the model was fitted with a 1600 engine but by the time it came into production in 1970 had gained the V8: otherwise much of

Right: Last of the Giulia derivatives, the Junior Zagato, built from 1970 to 1975 in 1300 and 1600cc form. Body was in steel so it was relatively

Below: The Montreal was based on the Giulia floorpan and was first shown at the 1967 World Trade Fair in Montreal. Hardly ever raced, despite having the Tipo 33's V8 engine, but here is Jon Dooley giving the car its UK racing debut in the 1974 Silverstone Six Hour Relay.

the car's componentry was straight out of the 105-Series parts bin. The general impression it conjures up is that of a highly-strung thoroughbred, although quite usable given a healthy bank balance.

Giulia Sprint Speciale.
Giulietta curves, with 1600cc

The Giulia Sprint Speciale was externally identical with the beautifully curvaceous Giulietta-based SS, but between 1963 and 1966 it was available in very small numbers, perhaps 1400 or so, with a tuned Veloce-spec 1600 engine unit. Initially employing three-shoe drum brakes, the SS was soon fitted with a Girling disc system at the front whilst retaining finned aluminium drums at the rear.

The fabulous TZs

The TZ 1, or Giulia Tubolare Zagato, was, like the GTA, intended as a road car as well as a racer, and in road trim it used the 1600 TI Super engine, (or similarly, SS with 45 DCOE Webers), canted over at such an angle that it required a special sump, gearbox bellhousing, intake and exhaust manifold. The front suspension linkage had been extended to improve handling - the lower wishbones were quite different; there was independent rear suspension, the rear discs were inboard, and the transmission was suitably beefed-up. An amalgamation of Zagato styling at its most breathtaking, rendered in lightweight aluminium panels, (a

small number were clad in glassfibre,) combined with an immensely rigid tube-frame construction, made for a very special car indeed, and with the absence of sound-deadening and creature comforts you were effectively driving a racer on the road. Only 112 road and race cars were made between '63 and '67 and the final 12 cars were clad by Zagato with much more aggressive looking GT bodywork in glassfibre. These were known as TZ 2s, were equipped with the GTA's twin-plug head and wide 13 inch diameter wheels and they enjoyed a small measure of success in events like the Targa Florio.

Junior Z. Small heavyweight

Lastly, there is the Junior Z. Perhaps the most surprising aspect of the Junior Z is that its body is panelled in steel like the 2600 SZ rather than alloy and, as such, is surprisingly heavy for a Zagato design. Taut-handling and nimble, the Junior Z was a good-looking car, with its full width plexiglass front and Kammtail. It seems to me that Giugiaro had similar ideas in mind when he penned the designs for the, admittedly, larger Alfetta GTV. A novelty aspect of the car was that it was possible to raise the rear hatch a fraction whilst in motion to improve airflow through the

car although, in practice, I can testify that a gap in the tailgate has the effect of drawing exhaust fumes into the car, having driven many miserable miles thus in a GTV6. I am assured that the arrangement in the Junior Z does work perfectly well. Built as a 1300 from 1970 to 1972, and as a 1600 from '72 to '75, there were 1108 of the smaller-engined version and just 402 with the larger unit. The 1600 is fractionally longer, has different rear lights and the petrol filler changes sides. It goes without saying that any of the Zagato-bodied cars are the province of the true connoisseur.

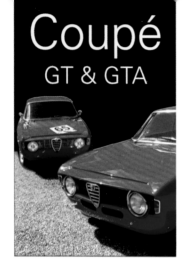

Coupé
GT & GTA

3

GTA
The Racer's
Coupé

Dott.Ing.Chiti, who masterminded the Autodelta operation.

Any motor manufacturer who participates in motorsport, whether as a publicity-seeking exercise or to "improve the breed" has its reputation bolstered to a great extent, provided there are some successes. This was all very well in the '60s, as William Boddy of *MotorSport* observed in April 1970, "Many of those who buy modern Alfas surely do so because of this great racing tradition ... I would go so far as to suggest that Mercedes Benz, Jaguar and Aston Martin have lost prestige, if not sales, by dropping out ..."

A racing heritage
Alfa Romeo's reputation for building brilliant racing cars was laid down in the 1920s and '30s with the P2 and P3 Grand Prix cars and the 1750 6C and 8C sports cars, and everyone knows Nuvolari beat the might of Mercedes and Auto Union at the Nürburgring in 1935 with the out-dated P3.

I was hooked on the marque as a little child, probably after the Tipo 159s of Farina, Fagioli and Parnell swept the board on their first visit to the UK in 1950, and thereafter I followed the exploits of maestro Fangio; the P158/9s were red, the bonnets were long, the grille looked right and they were exciting.

The company retired from world-class racing in 1953 following the failure of the 6C 3000CM sports cars to dominate in a way the Alfetta 158s and 159s had done in Grands Prix. Beautiful as these Colli-bodied machines were, and despite Fangio's 2nd place achieved with only one wheel steering, in the Mille Miglia in that year,

the management decided to quit and the competition banner was carried by privateers in production cars. At first, these were the Giulietta Berlinas and Sprints, of course, but to say production cars is slightly misleading because, as the decade wore on, it was the light, Zagato-bodied Giulietta SVZs and, from 1960, the SZs, which were amazing everyone with their agility and verve. These, and the lightweight Giulietta Sprint Veloces, were the precursors of the GTAs of the next decade, and their story is told in the excellent book *Veloce: the Racing Giuliettas* by Donald Hughes and Vito Witting da Prato (G.T. Foulis, England).

The birth of Autodelta
In 1962, the one-time Ferrari and ATS Technical Manager, Carlo Chiti, joined the Chizzola brothers, who ran an Alfa Romeo dealership, and assembled the Zagato-bodied TZ competition cars, which the Alfa factory had been developing from as far back as 1959. The Chiti/Chizzola garage operated under the name of Delta Automobili at Udine near Venice. The name was subsequently changed to Autodelta, and the company came under the wing of Alfa Romeo in 1964 when the Alfa directors decided to go racing again. Autodelta was moved to Settimo Milanese, a village just west of Milan, and had Dr. Chiti as General Manager and Roberto Bussinello as Sports Manager. With an engineering doctorate, Bussinello had been a test driver and development engineer for De Tomaso and he joined Alfa Romeo in 1963 in a similar capacity.

Newly restored 2000GTV, straight from Malcolm Morris' workshop.

It has sometimes been said that despite Dr Chiti's technical astuteness and engineering inspiration, the Autodelta set-up was deficient in administrative and organisational ability, and it was mainly for these reasons that it failed to achieve maximum potential ... All I can say is that Dr Chiti responded instantly when I put some questions to him in order to compile this chapter. Also it should be appreciated that in the '60s there was no real precedent for big-time professionalism in anything other than Formula 1 motor racing. In touring car racing, at least, Autodelta notched up some pretty impressive results.

The Tipo 33 sports-racing cars were not very successful, partly because things evolve constantly in prototype racing and the resources available were insufficient to keep up; and in GT events, the *Tubolare* Zagato TZ1 and TZ2 were reliable class winners in international events like the Sebring 12 hours and the Targa Florio in the early-to-mid '60s. Dr Chiti used to go to as many of the events his cars were competing in as possible, but if you consider that the 1967 calendar listed 72 such meetings he couldn't have been expected to get to them all. Perhaps overall Autodelta's resources were spread a mite too thinly?

Alleggerita! The original GTA

Although the GTA is usually thought of as a competition car, it was listed as a production model from 1965 to 1969 and would have cost you £2898 in 1966, nearly £1000 more than a regular Sprint GT, to which it was more or less identical in appearance. A mere 1000 of these homologation specials were produced, including variants, with only 50 in right-hand-drive, making them the most desirable of the 105-Series coupés. When the GTA was introduced at the Amsterdam Motor Show in 1965, few observers could envisage that Alfa Romeo would really produce a thousand units of what was clearly a spartan racing car.

However, the specification alone cannot justify the huge prices often asked nowadays for road-going GTAs, particularly when it is possible to get an ordinary Sprint GT for perhaps a quarter as much. Still, the serious collector will pay a high price for a GTA and this premium is a reflection of the low production run and the charisma of the racing association. An Autodelta

Far left: Early days of the European Touring Car Championship, with Giancarlo Baghetti's winning Giulia TI Super passing a pair of Coopers at the end of the banking at Monza, on 25th October 1964. Note the Saab and the Mini Cooper on the main circuit.

Left: Carlo Chiti in jovial mood at Brands Hatch.

Below: The TZ2 of Zeccoli/'Geki', third in the up-to-1600cc class in the Targa Florio of 1966.

Jon Dooley's 2000GTV charges through the 1976 Texaco Tour of Britain.

Right: Autodelta usually fielded four cars; here is the fourth-placed de Adamich/Galli car in the same 1967 Nürburgring race.

Below: The "A" of GTA stood for Alleggerita, *or lightened, due to its aluminium panels and plastic windows. This is Enrico Pinto at Monza in July 1966.*

car with provenance would be offered at a price nearer to ten times that of a Sprint GT.

The "A" of GTA stood for "Alleggerita", or lightened, as the model featured an aluminium-panelled body and plexiglass windows. The floorpan, inner shell and sills were the only steel sections. This conferred a weight saving of some 500lb, vital in a competitive situation where power-to-weight ratio is critical. Even mechanical components were in lightweight magnesium alloy, including the cam-cover, front crankcase cover, bellhousing and rear gearbox plate. A

few early Autodelta cars were fitted with plastic dashboard.

The GTA's twin-plug head endowed it with 115bhp at 6000rpm, which may seem only a modest gain over the standard 1600cc Sprint GT's 109bhp, but an Autodelta-tuned car with twin 45mm DCOE Webers and 10.5:1 compression ratio would yield at least an extra 50bhp at 7500rpm, when it could be doing 136mph. A significant increase in performance came when the inlet port sizes were reduced; the only difference between the Sprint GT and GT Veloce is the port sizes, and the cars were

found to run much better with smaller inlet ports. Racer Jon Dooley, editor of the Alfa Club magazine from '67 to '74, suggests that the discovery may have been made by accident when someone fitted a 1300 head by mistake; the 1300 port sizes were at the time the same as that adopted by the GTA and Sprint GT Veloce. It wasn't long before the 1300 GT also got smaller inlet porting.

In the early days of Autodelta, reasons for retirement during long distance events such as the Spa 24-Hours, were often reported as being due to piston failure. Now Ing. Chiti refutes

Below: Look at that grin! GTA and driver in their element: the Bianchi/ Rolland car was first overall in the 1967 Nürburgring 6-Hour race.

this, saying he doesn't recall this being the case, simply that all new cars had teething problems and they were still learning how to tune them and set them up properly; high-compression pistons were changed as a matter of course during engine rebuilds.

45

One of the Autodelta GTA's races through rain-soaked gloom in the 1966 Snetterton 500Kms.
Inset: The immaculate engine compartment of Toine Hezemans' GTA prior to the 1970 Tourist Trophy race at Silverstone in 1970.

Unlike the modern fuel-injected Alfa 75 Twin-Spark, with its silky-smooth power delivery, the GTA only had one distributor, and restorers note that this is now a rare item. The benefits of the twin plug arrangement are that it confers a more thorough combustion and smoother power delivery, and allows the use of bigger valves which couldn't be accommodated with a single, central plug. Also different from the standard specification are the 14 inch Campagnolo alloy wheels, as opposed to the Sprint GT's pressed steel 15 inchers, which allow fatter tyres, often Kleber Colombes, under the wheelarches; it was also necessary to fit smaller 266mm front discs to go with the 14 inch rims, and front spring rates were softer because the GTA was a lighter car. The exhaust pipes were of bigger bore, and there was a set of close-ratio gears. The interior was, appropriately, more spartan and rudimentary.

The GTA SA: forced induction for 220bhp!

Autodelta tried a supercharged version of the 1600 car, called the GTA SA. (SA - *sovralimentazione* - supercharge.) Shown at the 1967 Turin Sports Car Show, the GTA SA ran as a Group 5 car, which is to say highly modified, and its forced induction was evaluated at 2.2-litres, placing the model in the over 2-litre category. It was intended to blow off the Cosworth FVA-powered Lotus Cortinas and F2-engined BMWs. Apart from BMW, the GTA SA was the only supercharged car to compete in the European Touring Car Championship in the '60s.

Basically, the supercharging apparatus consisted of twin Fiat-made cabin blowers from an aircraft's ventilation system, installed ingeniously at each end of the air filter box. The compressor blades of each unit were driven by connected hydraulic turbines, themselves driven by a high-pressure oil pump mounted on the timing cover. The compressors pressurised sealed Weber carburettors via the central airbox. An oil cooler was mounted ahead of the radiator. The GTA SA's outright performance was restricted due to the need to run on regular fuel; the supercharged Alfetta 159s would have used a much more exciting cocktail. Nevertheless, the GTA SA gained on torque, produced 220bhp and was capable of 145mph. Autodelta stopped developing the GTA SA when the Championship regulations changed its categorisation from Group 5 to Group 2. To build 1000 supercharged cars would have been unfeasible.

Junior, the little GTA

The second derivative of the original GTA was the GTA Junior of 1968, and although only 447 were said to have been built, the true figure may be as high as 1000. It was introduced to contest the 1300 class of the European series, an area in which the Mini Cooper S was then dominant. The GTA Junior's 1290cc engine was an over-square version of the Giulietta unit (or you could describe it as a short-stroke version of the 1600 engine) with wider bore and shorter stroke and it, too, had the close ratio gearbox.

Despite the twin-plug cylinder head and fuel injection the Junior lacked the bottom-end torque of the 1600 car, but this was compensated for by the high revving engine once it was up and running. The 1300 GTA Junior really didn't start to come on song until it hit 5000rpm, and with a close ratio box it didn't feel particularly quick on the road. But in reality it was much quicker than it felt. Some 1300 GTA Juniors had limited slip diffs, but not all did, and the 1600 never had one ex-works.

Carlo Chiti believes that "On the whole, the GTA 1300 Junior was more reliable than the 1600 GTA and GTAm because its powerplant was of a smaller displacement in the same casing as the 1600 unit, and it used the same gearbox, suspension system and brakes as the 1600, and all things being equal, it made the 1300 GTA Junior a more robust car."

The Junior's interior was less austere than its larger-engined sister, and there was more soundproofing, which had a more civilising effect. Handling of both cars, GTA and GTA Junior, was of a very high order although, in a racing context, one-time Autodelta pilot and present-day suspension tuner Rhoddy Harvey-Bailey says the cars rolled badly, displaying that characteristic wheel-wagging in corners where several inches of daylight are visible under the inside front wheel. He observes that the Lotus Cortina did likewise, but the GTA was particularly prone to doing it. Basically, it was caused by having a soft rear, stiff front, suspension set-up, which was necessary to make the rear axle

48

work properly. *Motor* magazine's view of the GTA in 1966 was that it was "... everything a racing Alfa should be; fast, noisy and very stable. The steering was rather low geared which allowed arm flailing without affecting the direction of the car too much." In the same year, during a Silverstone test day, *Autosport's* John Bolster remarked that the GTA was "... at its best when all four wheels are sliding."

The inherent difficulty with any live rear axle is locating it, in a lateral sense, and a solution tried by Autodelta was the sliding block rear suspension. The locating pivot normally on top of the differential was moved underneath it, in order to lower the rear roll centre, and it moved within a vertical slot formed by brackets bolted onto the rear platform. This, according to Rhoddy, was a waste of time because it jams when under

The GTA 1300 Junior was more robust and reliable than the regular 1600 GTA, and it was European Touring Car Champion in 1972.

lateral load. Although it located the axle effectively from side to side, sliding on the differential casing, as a method of combatting the car's major problem which was keeping the roll centre

Capri sandwich! The 2-litre GTAm was based on the US-spec 1750 GTV. Here, Toine Hezemans leads on his home ground at Zandvoort, in August 1970.

down, it was a disaster. The front roll-centre was actually raised, lifting the outer top ball-joint in relation to the upright, and this served to maintain the camber angle on roll. The stiff front end, coupled with a soft rear, is what produced the strange roll axis, manifest in the wheel lifting during cornering. Autodelta persevered with the sliding block idea mainly because Carlo Chiti designed it.

Some people say Dr Chiti was a hard man to get on with and others testify to his geniality, but notwithstanding his personality, Chiti was always noted for designing complexities into cars. An example is the magnesium chassis tubes which also carried the fuel in the first Tipo 33, and his F1 car, the ATS, was very complicated. But he ran Autodelta efficiently enough during the GTA era, developing it from a collection

Autodelta used already homologated panels and mechanical components to create the GTAm. Hezemans won the Monza 4-hours of March 25th, 1970.

of Italian privateers like the Jolly Club. The Autodelta workforce numbered some sixty people, and there were never less than ten cars being prepared at any one time; Dr Chiti required of his mechanics that they be "passionately keen on motor racing, physically strong, competent, and able to work away from home a great deal." Although men with such attributes were hard to come by, there was no shortage of applicants, such was the draw of working at Autodelta.

Subsequently, the Jolly Club continued to run cars prepared for them by Autodelta, and in fact Autodelta assisted as many as ten or twelve private teams. Autodelta ran between four and six of its own cars from race to race, normally selling them off with a full overhaul to private customers after each season. Between 1965 and 1972 they used perhaps 50 GTAs of one sort or another. It was not possible to convert a 1600cc GTA to the later GTA Junior or GTAm because they would have had the chassis number stamped on them, and it could not be changed.

The GTAm, an American tale

The version known as the GTAm was brought out in 1970, based directly on the US-spec 1750 GTV. There is a little confusion about what GTAm stands for; some would have it that the "m" stands for "maggiore", or greater, which is to say, enlarged. However, the official version, which can be found in the Alfa magazine *Il Quadrifoglio*, October 1969, and indeed the contemporary homologation papers, is that the "Am" part is an abbreviation for "America",

because the car used a version of the Spica fuel injection fitted to US-specification cars. Autodelta GTAs had been using fuel injection since March 1968.

The 1750 GTAm is listed as a production car for 1970, so it was no problem to build the requisite 1000 units for homologation purposes. It looks identical to a standard 1750 GTV and so it is, even down to the steel body, but for the US-spec modifications. These thousand units are counted into the total production figure for 1750 GTVs and where things become confusing is that they only ever built 40 of the out-and-out racing GTAms; the way it worked was that you could specify any of the competition options when you ordered the car, in order to turn your purchase into a Group 2 racer.

These variations included cylinder heads, panels, plastic bumpers and the sliding block rear suspension. You could also gain access to the Autodelta settings to get your car into race trim. When Autodelta got their hands on the GTAm it sprouted flared wheelarches, which were in steel, with the original arches underneath cut away sufficiently to allow the use of wide slick tyres and Tipo 33 magnesium alloy wheels. This

arrangement appears quite crude today when, doubtless, a more comprehensive job would be done on the body. But back in 1970 things were a little more casual, and teams were still experimenting with ways to accommodate ever-increasing tyre sizes. Spoilers and air-dams on touring cars had yet to be seen.

Alfa Romeo had been looking at the possibility of going in for Formula 2, and the GTAm inherited the fruits of that research. The 1750 engine was bored out to 1985cc, using a one-piece casting for the four 'siamesed' cylinder liners; this was necessary because of the closeness of the bore-spacing. It used lightweight pistons, the narrow-angle *piccolo* head with four valves and only a single plug per cylinder. Remarkably, the head to block joint was metal to metal, with gasket sealer used only at the base of the cylinder liners. The GTAm notched up enough wins in the 2-litre class to take the 1970 Championship. The advent of the 2000 GTV engine allowed the GTAm to dispense with the siamesed liners, as it could now use the new bottom-end.

Track Superstar

In European circuit racing from 1965 to 1972 and even beyond, the GTA and its derivatives were pretty much

supreme in their classes. Autodelta had a rigorous training programme which centred on Alfa Romeo's Balocco Test Track, and according to Carlo Chiti involved 14 people testing from morning until night. On circuits like Spa and the Nürburgring, the GTAs generally excelled - provided they kept going - and Monza and Zandvoort were also Autodelta favourites. However, circuits with lots of tight bends like Brands Hatch or Oulton Park did not suit the car so well, although it could still meet the challenge in the early days from the Alan Mann Team's Lotus Cortinas and stout opposition from BMW 1600s, 2000tis and the occasional Porsche 911S. In fact, it wasn't until the advent of the Alpina and Schnitzer-tuned BMW

2002tiis in the late '60s and twin-cam, FVA and BDA-engined Escorts in the early '70s that the GTAs finally met their match; even then, the GTV 2000 in 'standard' Group 1 trim was still a reliable class winner.

The works Autodelta cars were piloted by drivers such as Jochen Rindt, Nanni Galli, Andrea de Adamich, Ignazio Giunti, Enrico Pinto, Theodoro Zeccoli, Spartaco Dini, Carlo Facetti, Toine Hezemans and Rhoddy Harvey Bailey, to name but a few. Private entries were also seen in the hands of heroes of the day like Lucien Bianchi, Rob Slotemaker and Gijs van Lennep. These were the halcyon days when top-line drivers like Jackie Stewart or Graham Hill stepped straight from a

Grand Prix car into a tin-top saloon or Group 6 sports prototype and just got on with racing it. Motor racing isn't like that any more and hasn't been since the mid-70s, when you could still see the likes of Amon, Peterson or Stuck racing BMW CSLs, or Fittipaldi, Stewart and Scheckter guesting in Capris. Today's sports car racing is slightly different, and it's not meant to be cynical to say that it's where the aces end up when they've finished with Formula 1.

The mid- and late-60s may have been the real glory days for the GTAs, when they were at their rawest and fighting hardest, but the cars were remarkably successful in the European Touring Car Championship right up until 1976. This success was mirrored

Left: The GTA's twin-plug head endowed it with 115bhp at 6000rpm in standard trim; an Autodelta-tuned engine was good for 175bhp. This unit has fuel injection which Autodelta used from March 1968.

Below:Autodelta drivers with T33: Galli, Dini, Giunti in pensive mood.

in the US, where GTAs were class B winners in TransAm sedan racing.

Racing the Giulia Coupé: what the drivers say ...

The main private Alfa competition effort in the UK was down to the Roger Clark team - with cars driven by brother Stan Clark, rallycross expert, and John Handley, formerly British Saloon Car Champion in the Mini heyday - and Jon Dooley, who competed on his own and with Ian Marshall.

Left: John Lyon trying hard to get back in shape at Brands Hatch in March 1974.

Below: John Handley (no. 68) and Stan Clark in the Penthouse 1600 GT Juniors going for the same bit of Woodcote, Silverstone 1974.

Dooley had started off racing a Giulia TI whilst at university, before clouting a bank and going on to race a Giulietta TI. Things started to get going for him in 1969 when the One-Make-Car-Club ran a meeting at Mallory Park and Dooley proposed a challenge race between Alfa and BMW. He managed to persuade Alfa GB to sponsor the prizes for the Alfa competitors, and in

an opportunist move asked PRO Barry Needham to lend him a brand-new 1750 GTV for the occasion. Luckily the importer's confidence was not misplaced, for Dooley won the race and handed the car back undamaged. As

One of the Roger Clark Team 2000 GTVs opposite-locking at Silverstone, 1974.

it turned out, the BMW team was so weak that only a single car was fielded, compared with 14 Alfas.

In 1971 Dooley bought a TZ and did some racing in one of the early classic car championships. Then he got a GTA to go with it, acquired largely by mistake. It was listed in a *Sunday Times* advert as a TZ, but Jon's call established that it was, in fact, a GTA.

The vendor was prepared to drop his price in view of the fact that the TZ was a more valuable car, and it changed hands for £1100 cash.

For the 1973 season, Jon went racing with a 2000 GTV, bought through his employer's staff purchase scheme, and installed a roll cage in what was a nice, shiny new car. By the end of the year he found he could stay with the

Jon Dooley won the Alfa-BMW Challenge at Mallory Park in a borrowed, brand new 1750 GTV: he returned it undamaged.

Even the Giulia Super can be made to lift wheels! Jon Dooley early in his racing career.

Roger Clark Team cars for the first half of the race until the brakes and tyres went off. After the race he drove it home, whilst theirs went on the back of the transporter. "Terrific value-for-money competition", recalls Dooley. They were allowed to use TB5 Michelins, a special stage tyre which suited the 14 inch wheel. Until the Alfas were permitted to use the TB5s, their performance had

Above: Adrian Bertorelli leads Ian Marshall through Russell corner, Snetterton 1975.

been a bit lacklustre because there wasn't a decent road tyre available for the 14 inch wheel. Dooley did a couple of races in the GTA fitted with the wheels and tyres from the 2000 GTV and found the car handled really well.

Jon remembers his GTA fondly. "It was a great little car. I sold it to my brother, and he's still got it. I was once in the GTA, with its spindly little tyres and F-registration [1967/8 in UK], sitting at lights on the North Circular Road. A 911 Porsche came up

Left: The 2000 GTV with competition mods also made a great road car, according to Jon Dooley.

alongside and the driver's eyes came out on stalks when this apparently aged Sprint GT left him for dead." Dooley's was a road spec car, one of the very few right-hand-drive cars; only about 22 were brought into this country out of 50 made. A few of them were used in racing, especially in the States, as right-hand-drive is worth a second a lap or so on a right-handed circuit because of better weight distribution. At the end of 1973 Jon sold the GTV and moved on to an Alfetta saloon. The GTV, with its competition mods, made a superb road car, according to Jon Dooley. He never took the engine apart; all he did was improve the air flow a little bit by fitting a left-hand-drive air filter box and pick up, and relocating the radiator overflow bottle. The right-hand-drive air box is just that, a box with no special entry.

On the other hand, the left-hooker has a long tube which picks up the air-flow beside the radiator, producing a bit of ram-air effect. The car also had different cam timing than standard, ostensibly for track use, which had the effect of giving an extra 1000rpm, using the standard cam. It produced a beautiful sweet-running engine, pulling 6000 in 5th, on the *Autobahn*, as they say.

Dooley sold the GTV to an Italian restaurateur, who drove it to Italy, seeing off various 3-litre BMWs on the way. After a routine service at an Italian dealers the entire staff were standing round it with the bonnet up and the cam covers off, trying to work out why it went so quickly.

The GTV 2000s reappeared again for the 1976 season, sponsored by Macinnes Amcron amplifiers, which was

Above: Jon Dooley and 2000 GTV on a night-time forest stage during the 1976 Texaco Tour of Britain.

particularly appropriate for the Radio 1 Production Car Championship. It was a two-car team, with Jon Dooley in one and Amcron MD Ian Marshall in the other. Bearing in mind tyre restrictions the GTVs were pretty fast, and there were plenty of dramas, such as Jon losing his lead at Oulton Park when Phil Dowsett came up behind him and shoved him into the barriers at Old Hall. Since it was Good Friday, there was a scramble to rebuild the car on the Saturday for a race at Snetterton on the Sunday, and the ebullient Gerry Marshall donated a bottle of

Top left: Peter Hilliard's GT 1300 Junior up on two wheels at the Woodcote chicane in the 1976 International Trophy Race.

Opposite: Jon Dooley heads two BMWs and a Commodore at Oulton Park, 1976. Shortly afterwards, he was shoved off into the barriers.

champagne for effort. The Alfa Dealer Team, whose key personnel included Jon, Leo Bertorelli and Michael Lindsay, was running Alfasuds at the same time in the British Saloon Car Championship, so in the throes of rebuilding the GTV the 'suds had to be transferred from Oulton Park to Thruxton to practice on the Saturday for a race on Easter Monday. Quite an achievement for an amateur set-up, and says Dooley, "Sometimes it felt as if we were running it from the side of the road."

Racing Fabrications looked after Ian Marshall's GTV, whilst Jon's was looked after partly by himself and partly by John Goodchild, along with Brian Rouse who was chief tester at Alfa GB. However, the operation foundered a little after Ian Marshall had a bad accident with his GTV on the Tour of Britain; he rolled the car and hit a substantial post on the first stage, and lost a bit of interest after that. Jon had a bad shunt with his car at Thruxton, clouting the Armco at the chicane whilst going backwards

at about 40mph, which bent the panel-work a bit. The main difficulty was again down to tyres, restricted to 175/70 x 14s, so the cars were terribly short on grip, compared with cars like the Opels and the BMWs which could run on relatively wide 195XWXs.

Rhoddy Harvey Bailey - Autodelta

Rhoddy Harvey Bailey was the only Englishman to drive for Autodelta, and he provides some interesting insights into his days with the team. That an English Jaguar racer should get to drive for a team which tended to hire the Italian stars is interesting, but it seems he simply heard that test drives were being held, got himself to Balocco, and ended up staying for four years. He was not without experience behind the wheel of a GTA, having driven Dereck Morgan's right-hand-drive car in 1966 in Mod-Sports events. He did one season with the car, and although the engine was 'knackered' it proved very chuckable. During his time at Autodelta he raced mainly GTAs, and

59

went testing with Teodoro Zeccoli, but there were outings in 33s as well. The GTA was tiring to drive in long races because all the weight was on the left of the car: the driver, fuel and battery were all on that side, and in that respect, a right-hand-drive car was preferable.

Racing a GTA was clearly no picnic. In 1968 Rhoddy drove the whole 500 kilometres at Snetterton single-handed, and recalls that the car was very 'wheely' and quite difficult to drive. The exhaust noise grew louder as the stub pipe under the passenger door became detached through repeated contact with the track surface, and all the while he had a hard time staying ahead of well-driven Cortinas piloted by the likes of Sir John Whitmore and John Miles, not

to mention a great deal of banging door handles with Dieter Quester's BMW. Controlling the GTA was difficult mainly because of the angle of roll in corners which made it necessary to back off because the car had two wheels in the air and was oversteering so all the while the driver was trying to balance the car to maintain the fastest speed. In another race at Spa, Rhoddy was allocated one of the early cars, which had a special aluminium floor pan, and this kept breaking up and having to be fixed. In one miserable race he 'stuffed' a GTA Junior at Brands Hatch, claiming he didn't enjoy driving it. The GTAm was a nicer car to drive because it was lower, and although it still waggled its wheels there was more rubber on the road.

Peter Hilliard at speed in the 2000 GTV on the Epynt section of the 1974 Tour of Britain.

Nowadays Rhoddy Harvey Bailey runs a thriving suspension tuning and handling business in the beautiful Derbyshire Dales, capitalising on long years of testing all kinds of road and race cars. Apart from his Rolls-Royce, Bentley and Range-Rover specialisations, he also puts his Alfa expertise to good use by fine-tuning the handling of such cars as the 75, which benefits from stiffer springs at the rear and a thicker roll bar at the front. He has recently sorted out the handling of the Montreal, famous for digging its nose in under braking, providing masses of understeer going

into a bend, wallowing through it, then oversteering on the way out.

There is an on-going development programme for the venerable twin-cam engine, with the classic saloon series in mind. Rhoddy owns a GTA virtually identical to his Autodelta car, which he hopes to air in certain historic events, although it is likely he will dispense with the sliding-block rear suspension. He also has a Giulia Sprint GT which is the test bed for his competition ideas, and which he plans to run in the Pre '65 series.

He offers an engine package for 1600 and 2000 Alfa units, from road-going to full-race, and there are a number of modifications which have been developed by his engine man Dave Whitehurst, a one-time expert on the Ford DFV Formula 1 engine. These mods centre on cams, new pistons, combustion chamber shapes, valves, and carburation for road use, with balancing central to the competition engines.

The engine, like the handling of the Sprint GT, presents a complex set of problems to overcome when higher performance is sought; even the GTA is not necessarily a satisfactory compromise for, in its day, a works GTA was a very different car performance-wise to a private GTA. Even in the pre- GTAm days the 1600 unit was only producing a modest 165-170bhp. Perhaps un surprisingly, the fastest of the GTA variants was the supercharged 220bhp GTA SA which, said the man who drove it, "... went like shit off a shovel". Using a 4.5 diff, he reckons to have seen 6800 on the rev-counter in 5th gear.

With the upsurge of interest in classic car racing, one or two people like Rhoddy Harvey Bailey are blowing the cobwebs off their GTAs to give them a welcome airing on the circuits. Alfa Romeo's own Scuderia del Portello regularly contests International Historic Touring Car events, and it is a real thrill to see the GTAs hard at it again and the standard of preparation today - judging by a meeting I attended recently at Zandvoort - is superior to how it was back in the 1960s. However, such is the value of the GTA now that to risk damaging one is bravery in itself. At a Club practice evening at Snetterton in 1988 I was trying out Brian Hammond's racing Alfetta, watching in the mirror as Richard Banks grew ever nearer in his GTA until, suddenly, he disappeared in a spectacular plume of flying soil into the infield at the difficult Sear corner. To say he was choked would be an understatement, but the car was mended to his usual impeccable standards and reappeared in 1990 to win the outright concours award at National Alfa Day.

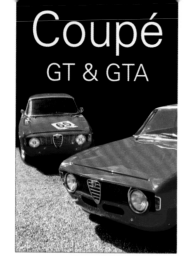

Coupé
GT & GTA

Right: 'Geki' Russo in the GTA at Monza, on April 25th 1965, when the car ran in the 1000kms as a prototype prior to homologation. The car behind is a Ferrari 250 LM.

Below: Giacomo 'Geki' Russo in conversation with Count 'Johnny' Lurani, then Vice President of the Automobile Club of Italy. Monza 1000kms 1965.

4

Track Record

The racing history of the Alfa 105-Series coupés could fill a book, therefore this has to be a substantially abridged history. Our coverage does include the highlights, however, and hopefully gives more than just a flavour of the coupé's exciting track record ...

1965: the GTA makes its racing debut

The GTA's competition debut was in the prototype class at the Monza 1000kms in April 1965, but one car failed with a blown head gasket, and Russo's car was relegated to last place with water in its fuel. GTAs also ran in the prototype category at the Nürburgring 1000kms and Mugello, but it was homologated by July 1965. At Karlskoga, Sweden, de Adamich bent his GTA's front suspension on a corner marker whilst attempting to out-drag four Lotus Cortinas into the first turn.

Jolly Club entries were withdrawn for the Spa 24-Hours in mid-July, but next came the Snetterton 500kms in August '65. This event set the tone for many to come, with Roberto Businello, racing under Mario Angiolini's Jolly Club banner, battling with the Alan

The Zeccoli/di Bono 1600 GTA won its class at Mugello in 1965.

Below: Uraguayan Carlos Lepro was winner of Class C and 3rd overall in the gruelling Argentine Gran Premio Internacional de Turismo of November 1965.

Mann-prepared Lotus Cortinas of Sir John Whitmore and Peter Procter. De Adamich's car had been rolled by Piero Corbellini after setting fastest practice lap, and a clash of personalities seems to have resulted in Angiolini firing de Adamich the night before the race. In any case, this was a three hour race and the closing stages were run in the gathering darkness, necessitating headlights. After leading for much of the race, Businello had to pit twice to get his car's rear lights seen to: dodgy Alfa electrics had struck again! Despite slow pit-work, he was able to close to within a minute of victorious Whitmore at the end of the race.

The GTA's quickly-established fame was universal. In Argentina in November 1965 the Gran Premio Internacional de Turismo attracted a vast entry of 331 diverse cars. The route covered 2632 miles and, allowing for rest periods, the event lasted 11 days. Of the 308 cars which started in Buenos Aires, a battered handful of just 63 made it to the finish. In third place was the Uruguayan driver Carlos Lepro with a GTA; he had taken advantage of the road sections to make up for what he lost on the rough stuff. In any case, it was remarkable that the car held together on such an arduous event. At the close of the 1965 season in Europe Bussinello was 3rd and de Adamich 5th in the Championship, with Alfa Romeo trailing behind Lotus Cortina in the 1600cc division.

Meanwhile, the fortunes of Alfa Romeo down-under were being looked after by Alec Mildren, who had a reputation for making his cars stick

together properly. Thus it was that his Giulia TI Super won the Sandown Park International Six-Hour race in the hands of Frank Gardner and Kevin Bartlett, a win inherited when Bussinello's GTA burned a piston and threw a con-rod. Both Alfas were well ahead of what might be described as an eclectic field at this point. Apart from Alan Moffat's Lotus Cortina the field consisted of Toyotas, Izuzus, and Holdens, of course.

1966. double "A", de Adamich and Alfa

The main event always has a curtain raiser, whether it's a Grand Prix or an endurance race, and the 1966 Sebring 12-Hours had a four hour saloon car dice as its supporting event. Frank

Carlos Lepro's GTA kicks up the dust on a twisty mountain section during the 1965 Grand Premio in Argentina. Notice the belt across the bonnet between the front wings to secure the lid.

The Carlos Lepro GTA pictured in the Argentine backwoods during the 1965 Grand Premio. The Monza cap fitted on Autodelta cars is clearly visible, and a non-standard large-diameter straight-through exhaust pipe is fitted. The photos were given to Dr Bernardo Martinez by Carlos Lepro's widow, Alma Moreno. Sadly, Carlos Lepro died in a road accident in Argentina in 1968. Bernardo has owned the car (AR# 613642) since August 2000 and, in summer 2002 it was in the throes of the restoration process. Body paint and detailing was entrusted to Roman Tucker in Lapeer, Michigan, while Jack Beck in Omaha, Nebraska, was working on the engine, transmission and differential. The car would be restored to the same appearance as shown here, with the race number 429. Completion was scheduled for the beginning of 2003, and Bernardo planned to race it in US vintage events.

66

Opposite - On Saturday, October 30th 1965, Carlos Lepro was first to arrive to Arrecifes at the end of the sixth stage. The distance from La Falda to Arrecifes was 762.6kms, and he made a blistering run on this stage to win his class and take third overall. This was the first GTA victory in an event sanctioned by FIA. However, apart from the Gran Premio of 1965, this GTA raced only three more times. In May 1966, it won at El Pinar, Uruguay, and in October at Mar-y-Sierras, Argentina, it came first in class and first overall out of 102 entrants. During the third race of the year, the Gran Premio of Argentina, it won the first stage, Pilar-Carlos Paz, but failed to qualify for the second stage in San Juan because it didn't get from the finish line to the Parc Fermée in the required time.

Jochen Rindt won the 1966 Sebring 4-Hour race in a GTA, rebuilt after Bussinello's practice battering.

Opposite - This photo was taken at 6.30am at the end of the first stage (78km) of the 1966 Gran Premio, between Pilar and Carlos Paz. This stage was run at night, and the Lepro GTA is pictured at Embalse Rio Tercero, Cordoba, with large spotlights on. As the first car to reach the Embalse, it is about to be cheered by the waiting fans, anxious to see the survivors of the night stage. Carlos Lepro won the stage from the Fiats of "Larry" and Carlos Reutemann by ten minutes, after five hours of racing.

Williams is reputed to have described Jochen Rindt as "the fastest man God put on this earth to drive a racing car", and it was Rindt who was the winner in a battered GTA, rebuilt after Bussinello had crashed it in practice. The two GTAs of Rindt and de Adamich, together with the Lotus Cortinas of Whitmore and Procter, demonstrated that European hot-shoes could threaten the big-engined Mustangs, Darts and Barracudas.

The mid '60s were the days when races were staged at what seemed impromptu venues. Long before the

Österreichring was conceived, one such was the Austrian Aspern airfield circuit near Vienna; the type of circuit where corners were marked out by straw bales. Disorganisation was rife, to the extent that you could only pick up your passes from inside the circuit, but that was difficult because the local police wouldn't let anyone in without one ... There was no Race Control, and only an umbrella as a scrutineering bay. Nevertheless, Andrea de Adamich led for the first lap and spent the rest of the race chasing Sir John Whitmore's Lotus Cortina in a bid to regain the lead. The two cars were

Nino Vaccarella gets into the GTA he shared with Enrico Pinto for the Jolly Hotels trophy at Monza in May '66. The headlamp bezels are taped in place.

enthusiast Willy Stenger, and run over a series of circuit events and hillclimbs. John Aley, of Aleybars (roll-cage) fame, provided the UK connection. Peter Nocker won this inaugural series in a 3.8 Jaguar, and in 1964 Warwick Banks in a Mini Cooper got the verdict after a lot of protesting from Saab and Ford whose drivers had scored equal points. For '65 Herr Stenger altered the system so that there were separate championships for three classes: up to 1-litre, up to 2-litres and over 2-litres. It was to be principally a manufacturers' championship, with the drivers' title accruing from the best four performances in each class. BMC's Competition Department was less than happy with the arrangement and withdrew, leaving the Abarth 1000s with a clear run.

Alfa Romeo's weapon of campaign then was the Giulia TI Super, the lightened and twin-Weber-carbed version of the regular TI saloon, and on long, fast circuits it was extremely successful; on tighter tracks, the lighter Lotus Cortinas were better and generally were piloted by more talented drivers. Both de Adamich and Enrico Pinto had made a name for themselves driving TI Supers, however.

In 1966 one of the rounds, counting for half points, was in conjunction with the European Hill Climb Championship at Mont Ventoux. The event was dominated by the works Porsche Carreras driven by Gerhard Mitter and Hans Herrmann, but the Autodelta cars of Bussinello, Pinto and Ignazio Giunti were on hand to challenge the Alan Mann Cortinas of Whitmore and Lucien Bianchi. Although Giunti had been

but a couple of cars length apart at the finish of the one hour race, with Dieter Quester's BMW 2000ti a steady third. The other GTAs of Bussinello, Teodoro Zeccoli, and Maurice Damseaux and Serge Trosch of the Belgian VDS team finished in the first ten. Lively, not to say riotous, post-race parties were the order of the day, and pranks were carried out in hotels of the kind which would come to be more commonly associated with the antics of rock stars. Examples include the introduction of a cow into the foyer of an hotel, and the waters of

the same establishment's swimming pool being dyed dark blue.

The Targa Florio was the kind of race which attracted a galaxy of cars ranging from the works Ferrari and Porsche prototypes to privately entered MGBs, the odd Glas 130A and, of course, the GTZs. Whilst the GTZs had a good run in 1966, the two GTAs entered fell by the wayside.

The Championship was a bit less structured around a strict calendar of circuit events then. It was instigated in 1963 by German saloon car racing

Nanni Galli gets it sideways out of Snetterton's Russell corner during the 1966 500kms.

practising for two weeks for the event, he couldn't manage to pip Whitmore's red and gold Lotus Cortina. There was 0.8 seconds between their times. Pinto was third fastest, with Bianchi next ahead of Bussinello.

More regular events on the Championship calendar were the Nürburgring Six-Hours and the Spa 24-Hours, both long-distance endurance races with driver pairings and both incredibly taxing on men and machines. The 1966 Nürburgring race was won by de Adamich and Zeccoli from pole position, ahead of two BMW 1800tiSAs and a Lancia Flavia Zagato, with Giancarlo Baghetti and Dieter Manzel fifth in another GTA. The Lotus Cortinas were running wider tyres, and their wheel bearings failed as a result.

At Spa in July 1966 there were hoards of GTAs; nine, in fact, of which five were Autodelta cars, but it was not to be a happy race for them. Driver pairings were Bianchi/Baghetti, Damseaux/De Keyn, de Adamich/Zeccoli, Pinto/ Demoulin, Trosch/Harris, Rolland/ Verrier, and Pizzinato/Koob. At the appointed hour, there was the sprint across the track to the waiting cars lined up in echelon by the pits, engines burst into life, and the race was on. A Mustang driven by 'Pat' and Tuerlincx led the way from a contingent of BMWs for the first six laps, but, by lap seven, Pinto's GTA had the lead and there was a bevy of Alfas switching places behind the two BMW 2000tis of Jacky Ickx/Hahne and Glemser/Willy Mairesse. Most cars were pitting every two hours, but the Autodelta cars were coming in every 90 minutes and this naturally had a

bearing on the lap charts. In six hours, say, the BMWs and the Mustang would have come in three times to the Alfa's four. For some of the GTAs, it didn't matter much for there was a spate of piston failures and the de Adamich car was delayed with overheating. As dawn broke, the leading BMWs and Alfas hit trouble: the Glemser/Mairesse car suffered a broken piston ring, and the GTAs of Bianchi/Baghetti and Rolland/ Verrier succumbed to piston failure. Now the Hahne/Ickx BMW led the GTAs of Pinto/Demoulin and Gosselin/Pilette, whilst further down the field class the four Alfa Benelux Giulia 1300TI saloons circulated in reliable, if none too swift, fashion. The race ran out in that order, with the BMW pit-crew having to change a holed radiator. They managed this in just six minutes, so the car only lost one of its four-lap advantage over the GTAs. The Autodelta mechanics were no slouches, mind you, for a GTA head gasket was changed in 18 minutes. By then, the third placed Gosselin/Pilette car was 19 laps ahead of the Mustang, but in endurance racing the whole time scale is vastly different to Grands Prix, let alone 10-lap clubbie sprints.

The powerboat race which was the Snetterton round of the Championship at the end of July '66 saw four out of six GTAs fall by the wayside. There

were four Autodelta cars for Rindt, Galli, de Adamich and Bussinello, with two Belgian Team VDS cars for Trosch and Damseaux. With Whitmore's Lotus Cortina on pole and Galli's GTA beside him, Rindt's GTA and Hahne's BMW behind, it looked like quite a tussle was in store. Jackie Stewart in the second Alan Mann Cortina was fifth in amongst the Alfas at the end of the first lap, but soon took the lead with Rindt right behind him. For a time Roy Pierpoint's Mustang looked threatening as he passed an Alfa every lap, but a dramatic piston failure ended his race in a cloud of smoke. After an hour's racing, Galli had pitted to have his brakes checked, and Rindt had been in to have a broken oil seal replaced in his car's rear axle. The order was Stewart, de Adamich, Hahne, Trosch. At this point Bussinello crashed heavily at Coram curve after hounding Hahne, and the car bust into flames. He was unhurt and the fire was quickly extinguished by the marshalls. Had they waited a few minutes, the rain would have done it for them, for the heavens opened. The Lotus Cortinas promptly slowed; Stewart spun and Whitmore was locking up his wheels under braking. Both pitted and demanded wet weather tyres.

Meanwhile, de Adamich piled on the pressure, and after two hours had lapped the entire field, demonstrating

A snapshot of one of the two GTA SAs entered for the Snetterton race in 1967. Both cars were shunted off into early retirement but Galli's GTA was faster than Graham Hill's Lotus Cortina in practice.

Far right: GTAs always went well at Zandvoort and here they get off to a promising start ahead of the 911, as the field of assorted Minis and Fiats, plus the odd BMW and Lotus Cortina, leaves the grid in the 1967 event.

complete supremacy in some atrocious conditions. The Hahne and Glemser BMWs were next up, with the Belgian GTAs behind them. Further down the order, the open-booted Fiat Abarth 1000s, in the hands of such as Toine Hezemans and John Fitzpatrick, were mixing it with the Lancia Fulvias and the 970S Mini Coopers of Paddy Hopkirk and Julian Vernaeve. With weather conditions worsening, cars were dropping out thick and fast. These included Galli, who hit a bank, Whitmore, who did the same, and then Rindt followed suit at Riches bend. Damseaux circulated slowly after deranging his GTA's back end, but de Adamich continued to progress in a smooth and unflustered manner to victory. Hahne finished on the same lap, with Glemser next, Stewart a few laps down in fourth, followed by Trosch; the first three cars were sounding as sweet as they had some four hours earlier. Despite the dreadful weather, de Adamich still managed to average 74mph.

So, in 1966 Alfa Romeo clinched the series with wins at Monza and Nürburgring (de Adamich/Zeccoli), Snetterton and Zandvoort (de Adamich) and Budapest (Pinto/Giunti). De Adamich was thus European Touring Car Champion. There were wins in GTAs for Rindt at Sebring and Frank Gardner at Lakeside in the Australian Grand Prix. Damseaux took a class win in the Coupé de Spa and later in the year Pinto/Demoulin were class winners in the Spa 24-Hours. At most of the SCCA events in the USA Gaston Andrey and Horst Kwech were outright winners;

the story was the same at events all over Europe.

1967: International success and another Championship for de Adamich

On 16th May 1967 the T33-3s sports prototypes of Vaccarella/Hezemans and de Adamich/van Lennep came first and second in the Targa Florio, with not a lot of serious opposition, it must be said, because the works Porsche 908s failed on the first lap; a lone GTA finished in 16th place, whilst the Sicilian crowd went wild with delight at an Alfa victory.

Autodelta management often found itself at loggerheads with circuit officialdom, even on the home front, for the four works GTAs were scratched from the 1967 Monza 4-Hours when the scrutineers demanded that the rear tyres, which stood proud of the bodywork, should be shrouded with spats or swapped for narrower rubber. Giancarlo Baghetti's GTA had been fastest in practice, ahead of Gerhard Mitter's works-backed 911, with de Adamich third quickest. With no Autodelta cars in the race, though, it

was almost a 911 benefit; the privately-entered GTAs of Massimo Larini/'Ans' and Artur Blank/Enzo Corti were third and fourth.

The Snetterton 500kms on Good Friday 1967 was a debacle for Autodelta, with both the promising GTA SAs of Galli and Bussinello being shunted off, one on the start-line, the other at the esses on the second lap.

Oulton Park turned out to be virtually a repeat of the 1966 wet Snetterton race. At Oulton the RAC Tourist Trophy was staged as part of the 1967 European Touring Car Championship, and again it was Andrea de Adamich who carried off the laurels, despite never having driven at Oulton before. Enrico Pinto and Rhoddy Harvey Bailey drove two other Autodelta cars, and they were all in the first of two heats. De Adamich and Harvey Bailey passed a spinning Pinto, and as the rain came down the Italian pulled away to take the chequered flag, breaking Jim Clark's long-standing lap record set in a works Lotus Cortina. Eyebrows were raised at the sight of what were, in road-going terms, GT cars, making the running in

saloon car racing: but the Championship was for 'Touring Cars', after all ...

In the TT final, de Adamich and Pinto started side by side in pouring rain. De Adamich quickly took the advantage but pressing hard were Karl von Wendt in a works-supported 2-litre Porsche 911, Giorgio Pianta in a similar car, the Mustang of Bo Ljungfeldt, the Camaro of Tom Lynch and Harvey Bailey next up. De Adamich was pulling away until an error of judgement sent him up the escape road at Cascades, and he lost several places in so doing. Gradually he caught up with von Wendt who had inherited the lead, and on lap 20 he took advantage of the traffic to pass the Porsche as they came up to lap back markers. Pinto finished fourth and Harvey Bailey, speeding up as he grew more accustomed to the GTA's handling, was sixth.

De Adamich went on to score maximum points in the Budapest Grand Prix, which was round six of the 1967 Championship, ahead of Nanni Galli with Teddy Pilette fourth. Pianta's Porsche 911 was third and von Wendt's was fifth.

Meanwhile, in the US TransAm Championship, Horst Kwech was busy mopping up the 2-litre class with his GTA, usually not far behind the leading Camaros, Mustangs, Cougars and the like. Others to do well in GTAs were Lee Midgley, Bert Everett, Gaston Andrey, and Harry Theodoracopulos. In a rather different world, in an endurance sports car race like the Daytona 24-Hours, naturally dominated in 1967 by the magnificent P4 Ferraris and Porsche Carrera 6s, a couple of private GTAs could be found at the tail end of the field, amongst the MGBs and Volvo 122s and TR4s.

Probably the most taxing event on the European Touring Car Championship calendar was the Spa 24-Hours, partly because the weather conditions always played such a significant part. A long, 8-mile circuit in the Ardennes, it could be raining on one side and dry on the other and, in the '60s, there were no car-to-pits radio links to warn drivers of what conditions to expect. Thus a car on dry tyres could hurtle full-tilt into a rain storm, often with disastrous consequences.

The Bianchi/Rolland GTA won the 1967 Nürburgring 6-Hours ahead of the Schultze/Schuller GTA and Stommelen's 911.

In 1967 there was both blazing sunshine and pouring rain, and the previous year's winners, Ickx and Hahne, led the race for six hours in a Mustang. Initially the Autodelta cars were up amongst the leaders and, when the Mustang went out, the Pinto/Cavallari GTA was third with von Wendt/Frohlich's 911 in the lead and the J-P Gaban/'Pedro' 911 second. The Porsches swapped places and, as the dawn came up, Frohlich's

Nanni Galli cocks a wheel during the 1967 Vienna Grand Prix at the rudimentary Aspern airfield circuit.

Right: The fourth-placed Dezy/ Quernette GTA leads the third-placed Mustang of Chasseuil/Bossuyt, during the Spa 24-Hours, 1967.

car's distributor disintegrated, having damaged the engine with its misfiring. Pinto/Cavallari were second, with Dezy/ Quernette's GTA now third.

Interest in the pits centred on the Trosch/Pilette GTA, which had undergone considerable surgery, to wit, new alternator, gearbox, clutch and, finally, head gasket, which had taken 33 minutes to replace. The Gaban/'Pedro' 911 extended its lead until the wiper motor packed up, allowing Pinto to catch up a lap as the Porsche pits worked feverishly to fit a manual wiper system, and the GTA was a mere 2 minutes 15 seconds behind as the chequered flag

1000kms. There was even a clean sweep at the Limbourg Grand Prix at Zolder when de Adamich, Teddy Pilette and Yvette Fontaine took the first three places. Victories in the Tourist Trophy at Oulton Park, the Budapest Grand Prix and Zandvoort gave the Championship to de Adamich again. Other notable successes were the Nürburgring 6-Hours (Bianchi/Rolland), the 500kms of Nürburgring (Schultze), the Benelux Cup (Wim Loos), a class win in the Spa 24-Hours (Pinto/Cavallari) and a win for the GTA SA at the Hockenheim 100 miles (Dau). In Venezuela Trevale's GTA took the Caracas 6-Hours and Albert Poon won the Macao Grand Prix in Hong Kong. Giunti was European Hill Climb Champion in the Touring Car category.

1968: mixed fortunes and strong competition

The Monza 4-Hours was established as the season's opener by 1968 and the European series regulations changed to Group 5 rules which, broadly, allowed for more extensive modifications than the nearer-standard Group 2 rules.

There were two separate four hour events. The first for cars up to 1-litre, which comprised the Fiat Abarth 1000TCs against the Cooper Ss, and the second race for cars up to 2-litres. The latter was split into two classes, with the GTAs versus the odd Fulvia HF and 1600 BMW in the up-to-1600 group and all 911s in the 2000cc category.

The GTA SA of Lucien Bianchi was fastest in practice, but the car's handling and brakes didn't look like matching its devastating straight-line

fell. GTAs took the first three places in the 1300-1600cc class.

Unfortunately, the race was marred by a tragedy. During the night Dutchman Wim Loos spun his GTA into a tractor and then an electricity pylon beside the Masta straight, plunging the area into darkness and thus tragically impeding his own rescue. Despite the best efforts of the mobile Grand Prix Medical Service, whose transporter was behind the pits, Loos died in the helicopter en route to Liege hospital. As it was, the GP Medical Service saved the life of De Keyn, who had been extricated from his crashed GTA at

the same point on the Masta straight shortly before Loos went off. There had also been a considerable amount of panel bending among the droves of 1600 GTVs and 1300 GT-Js running in Group 1. Fatalities were not uncommon in the '60s, for seatbelts and roll cages were as yet not compulsory and Armco crash barriers were the exception rather than the rule.

GTAs were well into their winning stride all over the world and major wins included the Monza 4-Hours (Massimo Larini), the Vienna Grand Prix (Nanni Galli) and Trosch, Fontaine and Dezy filling the podium at the Chimay

Sicilian hero Nino Vaccarella drove GTAs on occasion; he was 5th at the Nürburgring in 1968.

Opposite bottom: Nanni Galli slides round one of Brno's strawbale-lined corners; he was second to de Adamich in 1968.

speed. The works GTAs, on the other hand, now with fuel injection, looked better bets for reliability and drivability over a long-distance race. And so it worked out for, despite leading for much of the first two hours, Bianchi retired with a broken throttle linkage, whilst the other two GTA SAs in the hands of Gerd Schuller and Giancarlo Baghetti were both totalled comprehensively. Nevertheless, there were sufficient GTAs left for Alfa to take the first three places.

The annual outing to Snetterton could have been a wash-out for Alfa Romeo, for the Autodelta transporter was involved in an accident en-route to the circuit and only one car was serviceable. Rhoddy Harvey Bailey drove it single-handed for the full 500kms, winning his class and coming 5th overall after some fearsome door-handling with Quester's BMW.

For the 1968 Nürburgring Six-Hours Alfa Romeo entered virtually every car they could muster. The two supercharged cars of Schultze/Bianchi and Giunti/Galli recorded practice times which looked good enough for outright victory, but such was the pace set by the Porsches and BMWs around the testing 14-mile circuit that hardly a single GTA was on form by the finish: the car of Mario Casoni/Nino Vaccarella was fifth, a lap down behind the 2002s

The Monza 4-Hours of March 1968 opened the season for the European Touring Car Championship; the GTA SA of Bianchi was fastest in practice but its handling and brakes didn't match its straight-line speed.

and 911s. Even the Broadspeed Escort 1300GTs weren't far behind.

The man at the Belgian weather shop had clearly emerged from his bed on the wrong side: the 1968 Spa 24-Hours was dogged with a complete repertoire of precipitation, including thick mist, drizzle, and pouring rain. Things were in a state of flux again with regard to the categories of cars going for the Championship. Out of 56 entries, 21 were Group 5 cars, 18 were Group 2, and 17 Group 1; these cars ranged from quite highly modified, through modified, to 'standard' road-going. The Alfa Romeo entry in Group 5 was the supercharged GTA SA for Pinto/Demoulin, and there were two Alfa Benelux GTAs in Group 2, and four 1750 Berlinas in Group 1.

Pinto's GTA SA sped off into a healthy lead from a couple of 911s, until the rain got heavier and he had to rush into the pits to demonstrate that his wipers had given up. At this point the Pilette/Slotemaker GTA took over in the lead, and when the race was an hour old, the visibility was sufficiently poor for the clerk of the course to ask for foglamps to be switched on by displaying the "Phares" sign. They were racing with 75-yards visibility ... Still, conditions change quickly in the Ardennes and, during the evening, there was just rain to cope with. By midnight the GTA SA was on

its last legs, having had trouble with wipers, plugs, ignition, and finally, the fuel pump. The Kremer/Kelleners/Khausen Porsche 911 went into the lead from Pilette/Slotemaker's Alfa GTA, and the Mini Cooper S of Vernaeve/Baker was third at this point from the 'Elde'/Duprez Mustang.

24 hours is an exceedingly long time to keep a car going, but the leading Porsche never missed a beat and at midday the order was Porsche, Mustang, Porsche, Alfa. The first three cars were running in Group 5, whilst the GTA was in Group 2; the first Group 1 car was the Lagae/Brel 1750 Berlina down in 18th place and 29 laps in arrears. In the closing stages, with

Right: GTAs featured prominently in South African Touring Car races as well as running in the sports-prototype events; here is the Basil van Rooyen/ Dave Charlton 1750-fronted car.

Below; Giorgio Pianta went well in 1968; he was teamed with Galli and Zeccoli. Note the GTA's pop-riveted rear arch flares.

just an hour and a half to go, Pilette's GTA broke its crankshaft, but to the adulation of the fans it continued to circulate to the end at about 10 minutes a lap. It had rained for 23 out of 24 hours!

An event guaranteed to warm the heart of Alfa fans everywhere was the classic Mugello road race, run over 66kms of picturesque Tuscany countryside in mid-Summer. In 1968 it was a straight fight between the Alfa 33s and Porsche 910s, and the tifosi went wild as the Bianchi/Vaccarella/Galli car beat the Siffert/Steinemann Porsche. The point of mentioning this is that you could have cars like the GTA running in the GT category alongside the very much faster sports prototypes. Theoretically, fans could bask in an outright Alfa victory having also delighted in the wonderful diversity of machinery on the road: Chevron B8 to MGB and Sprite, from Duetto to Fulvia, from 911R to GTA. The GTAs were also well up in the results, with Pinto's 1300 Junior sixth overall, ahead of Riccardone/Radicella's 1.6 GTA.

On Brno's strawbale, kerb and lamppost-lined streets - not to mention the unprotected race fans - the GTA SA of German driver Axel Sommer was fastest of the GTAs in qualifying, but in the race the regular drivers Zeccoli/ Giunti and Pianta/Galli were superior. They finished fifth, sixth and seventh behind BMWs and Porsches, with Roberto Bussinello dictating the order of the first two GTAs, despite the fact that the Pianta/Galli car was ahead of the other for most of the race. At this stage, though, there was still a good

Below: Gianluigi Picchi's red GTAm comes up against some heavy metal on his way to a class win at Zandvoort in August 1970.

chance that Zeccoli could win his class in the Championship. Unfortunately, they really messed up at the final round, a three hour event at Jarama, by pairing Zeccoli with Pianta, not realising that a shared drive in a race of less than four hours did not count for Championship points ... Curiously,

Right: GTA Junior keeps ahead of an Alpina BMW during the Brno Grand Prix, 1970. Softer front suspension settings were tried at the time in order to keep the outer wheel vertical; there was less wheel-waving as a consequence.

Opposite bottom: Hezemans' GTAm roars through the streets of Brno during his victorious Championship run. Imagine the noise as the bark of the engines bounces off the buildings!

all other entries were for single drivers and, again, the extra ccs of the 911s and 2002s ensured their domination of the race. A surprised Cooper S driver, John Rhodes, took the Championship class honours.

For the British Touring Car Championship you needed a Ford Falcon to ensure outright victory, whilst an Escort FVA would do for 1600 class honours. GTAs were rare in '68 and Geoff Breakell's car was usually down amongst the Minis.

In summary 1968 got off to a good start with the GT Sprint Veloce of Labaune/Cazal taking the Group 1 honours in the Monte Carlo Rally. The Monza 4-Hours was becoming GTA property with a class win (Division 2) for Pianta. Basil Van Rooyen won the South African Group 5 race at Kyalami and John French's GT Sprint Veloce won the Surfers Paradise 4-Hours in Australia. Rhoddy Harvey Bailey was class winner and 4th overall at Snetterton. Demoulin's GTA SA won the Grand Prix de la Frontiere at Chimay and Weizinger's GTA Junior took the up to 1300cc class in the Nürburgring 24-Hours. Pilette took the 1600 class win in the Spa 24-Hours.

1969: middleweights do best
By 1969 it was becoming clear that the GTAs were not cutting it in the up to 2-litre class, for they were up against increasingly reliable 911s and Escort twin-cams, and the BMW 2002tiis, now toying with Bosch turbochargers. The GTAs had by now been around for four years and the racing world was much more interested in the new BMWs.

The Guards Six-Hours at Brands Hatch in June 1969 was a victory for one of the BMW 2002tiKs of Hahne/Quester, although circuit knowledge and driver talent had a 1300cc Broadspeed Escort GT of Trevor Taylor and John Fitzpatrick in the lead at one point. The leading Quester/Hahne BMW wouldn't start from a pit stop, and a battery change put it back behind the Escort. Then it was a matter of waiting for the turbocharged car to catch the baby Ford. Otherwise, the main action centred on the BMWs of Chris Craft/Dieter Basche and Helmut Marko/Dieter Glemser, against the Rolf Stommelen/Geog Loos and Hezemans/van Lennep Porsche 911Ss, with an initial strong challenge from the Frank Gardner/Tom Belso Escort Twin Cam. There were only two Autodelta cars running: a GTA Junior for Pinto/Harvey Bailey and a fuel-injected GTA for de Adamich/Spartaco Dini. The GTA challenge faltered when de Adamich's car's throttle spring snapped and he spent 40 minutes fixing it just in order to get back to the pits, where the car lost a further hour while they repaired it.

The Spa race in 1969 could not have the traditional Le Mans type start because Armco had sprouted up everywhere, including the front of the pits where the cars used to line up. The four GTA Juniors present were matched against the BMC works Cooper S cars, and this developed into a straight fight between the Damseaux/Berger GTA Junior and the Cooper S of John Handley/Roger Enever; the Cooper had battery problems and fuel vaporized during a pit stop, whilst the Alfa had a leaking radiator. With about an hour

and a half left, the Cooper engine failed, leaving the GTA Junior to win the class and take 8th place overall. The race winner was the 911 of Guy Chasseuil/Claude Ballot-Lena, and the closest car to the Alfa in its class was a Renault Gordini which was 27 laps behind. This was to be the final appearance of the BMC works Minis, for with the Leyland takeover the Competitions Department was closed down, and with it went the GTA Junior's potentially most formidable opposition. Although Dini was European 1600cc-Class Champion, it was also the last year that the regular 1600 GTAs were to feature, as Autodelta was putting more effort into the 1300 and 2-litre categories.

A round-up for the year shows that Spartaco Dini was outright winner of Division 2, the up to 1600cc class in 1969, and Enrico Pinto was 1st in Division 3, the up to 1300cc class. GTA wins came at Monza, Vienna, Budapest (Dini), Nürburgring (Dini/de Adamich), Belgrade, Jarama (Giunti) and GTA 1300 Juniors won at Monza (Pinto/Larini), Budapest, Zandvoort (Pinto), Brno (Rosinsky), Nürburgring (Casoni/Zeccoli), Jarama (Facetti) and Marchairuz - Switzerland (Moscatelli). GTAs were also National Champions all over Europe and took sundry other events such as the Tour de France (Junguenet/Desagnat) and 1750 GTVs were class winners in the Kylami 9-Hours (Abrahams/Marais), plus the Bathurst 500 (Bartlett), to name but a few.

1970: the GTA makes its debut
1970 saw the appearance of the 2-litre GTAm, and the model took three out of

the first six places at the Tourist Trophy at Silverstone in June, followed by a straight one-two-three at the Nürburgring Six-Hours in July. Driver pairings were de Adamich/Gianluigi Picchi, Dieter Mohr/Hans Hessel, Teodoro Zeccoli/Christine Beckers, and Alfa Romeo made much of the girl-racer aspect in their advertising at the time.

What must by now seem to be a race in which only masochists participate also serves as a yardstick of reliability and consistency. The Spa-24 Hours of July 1970 contained the usual amount of appalling weather, and this year it was the seventh round of the Championship. The four Autodelta cars were handled by Demoulin/Claude Bourgoigne, Hezemans/Larrousse, Pinto/Berger and Zeccoli/Facetti. The opposition consisted of a works team of Wankel-

Below: The light blue GTA Junior of Scuderia Brescia Corse driven by Uberti/Zuccolo leads the orange National Dutch car of Han Ackersloot during the 1970 Tourist Trophy at Silverstone. They were fourth and third in class respectively.

Bottom;:Toine Hezemans was second overall in the 1970 Tourist Trophy at Silverstone after a finely judged second heat when he managed to go the distance without refuelling.

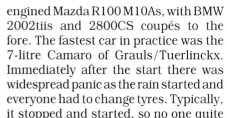

engined Mazda R100 M10As, with BMW 2002tiis and 2800CS coupés to the fore. The fastest car in practice was the 7-litre Camaro of Grauls/Tuerlinckx. Immediately after the start there was widespread panic as the rain started and everyone had to change tyres. Typically, it stopped and started, so no one quite knew which tyres to choose.

After a little over an hour the Camaro had lapped everyone, Pinto had suffered a jammed throttle linkage when lying eighth and the Hezemans car had blown its engine. The Camaro fell back as night drew on, one of the remarkable Mazdas was second and Pinto was back up to fourth. As morning came, this car was challenging the third place Mazda, and by midday the positions were reversed. The leader now was the Gunther Huber/Helmut Kelleners Alpina-BMW 2800, running with a 3-litre engine, and when the second place Mazda blew its engine at 2pm Pinto was elevated to second, two laps behind the BMW. As the remaining Mazda dropped out with ignition problems, the two other GTAs moved up to finish third and fourth.

Toine Hezemans captured the European Touring Car series with the 1750 GTAm and Carlo Truci took Division 2 with the GTA 1300 Junior. Outright wins were at Monza, Salzburgring, Budapest, Brno, Jarama (Hezemans), Nürburgring (de Adamich/Picchi), Zandvoort (Picchi) and 2-litre class honours at Silverstone (Hezemans) and Spa (Pinto/Berger). Division 2 and 1300 class wins were at Monza (Truci/Ghigo), Salburgring (Uberti), Budapest, Brno (Truci), Nürburgring (Truci/Facetti), Spa

80

(Dezy/Pizzinato) and Jarama (Galli). It was a similar story in national events all over the world such as the Tour de France (Pianta/Alemani 1750 GTAm) and the Malaysian Grand Prix at Kuala Lumpur and the Singapore Grand Prix, both won by Poon's GTA.

1971: Picchi and Hezemans take the Championship

Gianluigi Picchi scored maximum points for Alfa in 1971, winning the 1000-1300cc Division 1 with six out of eight rounds; his GTA Junior took Monza, Salzburg, Brno, Zandvoort, Paul Ricard and Jarama. Picchi was partnered with Guy Chasseuil at the last two races.

Massimo Larini/Luigi Colzani were class winners at Nürburgring, and it was the GTAm of Toine Hezemans/Carlo Facetti which won its class at the Spa round, the most prestigious of all dates on the European Touring Car calender. Indeed, Hezemans had nearly as many

A victorious John French waves his wheels at an astonished marshall at Lakeside, Queensland, Australia, June 1970.

successes as Picchi, taking Division 2 at Monza, Brno, Spa, Zandvoort, and Ricard. John Fitzpat- rick's Escort RS beat him in Austria and Spain, whilst the big league Division 3 was being fought out between the Cologne RS Capris and Schnitzer and Alpina BMW 2800 CSs. By virtue of class wins in Divisions 1 and 2, Alfa Romeo took the 1971 Manufacturers' title.

Most glamorous GTA Junior driver was undoubtedly Liane Engeman, who was third in class at the Brands Hatch Motor Show 200 in October. If Ms Engeman was the most glamorous driver, the award for the most spectacular driving demonstration of the year must go to Nanni Galli in the Tourist Trophy at Silverstone. The inside of Woodcote bend was marked

out with cones in those days, and Galli took down every one of them with his right-hand front wheel, which was hanging in the air in characteristic pose as he took the corner. He performed the trick not only on the first lap of the first heat, but repeated it in the second heat as well.

On the UK club-racing scene in 1971 the Alfa 'B' team of assorted road-going Giulias won the 21st 6-Hour Relay, an event run by the 750 Motor Club in which the widest spectrum of machinery participates. The following year they managed second behind the Porsche Club GB team.

1971 was the year of complete domination as Gianluigi Picchi and Toine Hezemans tied for first place in the Driver's Championship. Victories in Division 1, now the up to 1300cc class, occured at Monza, Salzburgring, Brno, Zandvoort (Picchi), Paul Ricard 24-Hours, Jarama 4-Hours (Picchi/ Chasseuil) and Nürburgring 6-Hours

Left: Gianluigi Picchi with his 1300 GTA Junior. Perspex side windows featured relatively sophisticated opening sections.

Below: Champion of 1971: Toine Hezemans, who took Division 2 with the GTAm.

Below: Picchi/Chasseuil won their class in the Paul Ricard 24-Hours of 11th/12th September 1971.

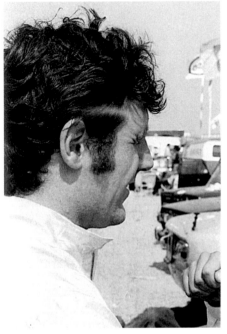

Left: Most glamorous Alfa driver in 1971 was Liane Engemann; here she is in a contrived pose on a motorshow stand.

(Colzani/Larini). Wins for the 2000 GTAm in Division 2, now up to 2 litres, were Monza, Brno, Zandvoort, Paul Ricard (Hezemans), Nürburgring (Hezemans/Van Lennep) and Spa 24-Hours (Hezemans/Facetti). GTAs and their derivatives were once again hugely successful in national championships: Austria, Belgium, France, Germany and Italy all had a host of Alfa winners and, in Spain, the GTAms of Barrios and Lopez were dominant. In the USA the SCCA Championship Class C went to a GTA 1300 Junior (Davenport) and outright winner of the Venezuelan Championship was a GTA (Spadaro).

Below: The GTAm of Facetti/
Hezemans finished fifth in the Monza
4-Hours of March 1972. A 1300 GTA
Junior fared less well ...

1972: the year of the GTA 1300 Junior

The Levis-sponsored European Touring Car Championship was held over nine rounds in 1972 and, in the up-to-1300cc category, the GTA Juniors swept the board in every one of them in what looked like a repeat of the previous year's series. The reliability demonstrated by the cars is no mean achievement and shows what six or seven years of racing development can do.

Autodelta, under Team Manager Johnny Marelli, was decidedly coy about the GTAm's ability to match the Escort RS and BMW 2002tii. Part of the problem was the weight factor, in that the regulations now stipulated glass instead of perspex windows and steel bonnet and boot lids instead of glassfibre or alloy: the GTAm was probably conceding 2cwt and 20bhp to the 1600 BDA-engined Escorts.

At the 1972 Championship's first round, the Monza 4-Hours, there were Autodelta GTAms for regulars Picchi/Zeccoli, de Adamich/Vittorio Venturi, Facetti/Hezemans, with two GTAms entered by the Jolly Club for Georg de Bagration/Raffael Barrios, Carlo Giorgio/Lella Lombardi. There were no less than 25 GTA Juniors entered, including three Autodelta cars, and it was one of these, driven by Luigi Rinaldi and Luigi Colzani, which saved Alfa's bacon by coming home sixth overall and winning its class. The fifth placed Facetti/Hezemans GTAm was completely outpaced by the Boreham-prepared 1800cc Escort BDA of Gerry Birrell/Claude Bourgoignie. A curiosity item of the race was the singular Alfa

Below: May 1972 and Picchi was outright winner at Brno in his 1300 GTA Junior. The win was marred, however, by the death of Luigi Rinaldi.

Bottom: Vincenzo Loda's GTA Junior leads Umberto Grano's Scuderia Filipinetti Fiat 128 round the streets of Brno in May 1972.

2600, with an even more curious driver pairing rejoicing in the names "Bloody Black Tiger"/"il Ragno", which actually managed to finish 13th behind the Giorgio/Lombardi GTAm!

Although privately entered GTAms sometimes picked up class wins through reliability, Autodelta themselves gave up on the GTAm for the time being and concentrated on the smallest, up-to-1300cc class. In the event, the Fords which threatened the GTAms and which promised so much at Monza were not that reliable; they only just took the up to 2-litre class from BMW, who hadn't gone for it with real seriousness. However, Autodelta's plan paid off again with the GTA Junior annihilating the minimal opposition and winning the series by virtue of most class wins.: Toine Hezemans, Gijs van Lennep, Carlo Facetti, F3 star Gianluigi Picchi, Spartaco Dini, (masquerading as 'Paco'),

Dutch champion Wim Boshuis, Austrian journalist Harald Ertl, Teodoro Zeccoli, Masimo Larini and Luigi Colzani, amongst others, all drove the cars, with the loss of Luigi Rinaldi at Brno. Drivers competing in the small-capacity class didn't qualify for the Drivers' Championship, but Facetti scored most points during the season.

Some will argue that the works 3-litre Cologne Capris deserved the Championship because they were always having to vanquish the big BMWs, whereas opposition for the Alfas came only in the shape of the Mike Parkes-run Scuderia Filipinetti Fiat 128s and some privately-entered NSU TTs. The Boreham Ford Escort 1300GT was no match for the GTA Junior, and Ford Cologne was intent on victory with the Capris. At the end of the day, only five points separated the Fords from the Alfas ...

Three of Autodelta's Group 1 2000 GTVs finished in the top ten at Spa in 1972 out of nine GTVs entered, with rally stars Jean Ragnotti/Jean-Claude Andruet swapping places with Claude Ballot-Lena/Jean-Claude Lagniez for much of the time. The latter finished as high as sixth which, on the face of it, was an astonishing achievement for what was virtually a road-going car, but you could also argue that it is not as highly stressed as a Group 2 car and thus more likely to go the distance. Whatever, it proved the car's reliability once and for all and it was fitting that Autodelta again won the Coupé du Roi team award. The Group 1 GTVs ran on Michelin racing tyres, whilst the GTA Juniors were Firestone-shod. In the final results the rest of the GTVs filled the upper midfield places, ahead of the GTA Juniors, in fact, the best of which was 21st.

At Silverstone for the Tourist Trophy the four Autodelta cars were augmented by the Swedish Topcon cameras team, with three national stars, Segring, Steenberg and Rothstein, having their first outing in the European series. The race was in two 2 hour heats, and there was much rivalry and place-swapping between the Italians, with Facetti the fastest, Dini and Picchi lapping together, whilst Larini diced at length with the Swedes. Facetti was sixth overall in heat one, and Picchi was ninth in the second heat. Overall, Facetti was 1300 class winner.

The picture was much the same at Jarama, where the GTA Junior of Hezemans/van Lennep started from the third row, only a matter of 8 seconds down from the pole position RS Capri of Glemser/Soler-Roig, and the Dutchmen were fourth overall. Having logged most class wins during the year, Alfa Romeo took the title outright.

In the UK in 1972 former Saloon Car Champion John Handley and Stan Clark ran 2000 GTVs in both Britax and Castrol sponsored Championships. Class divisions were, curiously, separated according to the value of the car, bearing in mind the Championships were for Group 1 cars. In the event, the Capris and Camaros were too fast for the Alfas, and Roger Bell's 2002tii was overall Champion. The GTVs improved in the second half of the season when they switched to TB5 Michelin tyres.

Far left: The massed ranks of Alfas on the grid at Spa, July 1972. Three of the Group 1 GTV 2000s finished in the top ten, and Autodelta won the King's Cup team award for the third time.

Left: All nine 1300 GTA Juniors in the 1972 Silverstone TT, including the Swedish Topcon team, ran with 13 inch wheels, glass windows and the narrow-angle cylinder head.

Centre: The GTA Juniors of Facetti, Picchi and Larini circulated in formation during the 1972 TT.

Bottom: Stop me and buy one! Roger Clark negotiates the Thruxton chicane in the Leo Bertorelli GTAm.

This was the year of the GTA 1300 Junior when Alfa Romeo took the title by virtue of total supremacy in Division 1. The roll of honour went: Monza 4-Hours (Colzani/Rinaldi); Salzburgring, Silverstone 4-Hours (Facetti); Brno (Picchi); Nürburgring 6-Hours, Paul Ricard (Picchi/Facetti); Spa 24-Hours ('Paco'/'Pooky'); Zandvoort 4-Hours ('Paco'/Boshuis) and Jarama 4-Hours (Hezemans/Van Lennep). The Giulia coupés, now including 2000 GTVs, and Supers continued to dominate the national championships from Belgium to El Salvador. Major successes included the Vienna Grand Prix (Marko, 2000 GTAm), the Nürburgring 300kms (Bertrams, GTA 1300 Junior) and the Mantorp Grand Prix (Steenberg, GTA 1300 Junior). Stateside, Kwech was now running a 2000 GTV and in the winner's enclosure again.

1973-1977: younger opposition and changing rules but the Giulia fights on

John Handley and Stan Clark won the Manufacturers' award for Alfa Romeo in the 1973 Tour of Britain, and perhaps the best irony was the Roger Clark Team's victory in the BMW Raceday at Brands Hatch in 1973.

Meanwhile, continental Europe witnessed a great upsurge of interest in Group 2 as the two German giants fought for outright honours once again. When the BMs sprouted wings in mid-season,

An Autodelta wheelchange, Silverstone 1973. Facetti's GTAm goes from wet to dry tyres at the last minute: it looks as though the quick lift jack didn't give enough wheel clearance.

it was virtually all over, such was their aerodynamic advantage. The GTAm was a class winner through reliable running at the opener at Monza, and it was the beginning of a minor renaissance for the car. Dini/Facetti were fourth at Salzburgring, and, to the amazement of the touring car establishment, again at the Nürburgring 6-Hours. This was in the company of the likes of Niki Lauda in a 3.5-litre BMW CSL and Jackie Stewart/Emerson Fittipaldi in a 3.0-litre Capri RS. They were only four laps down on the winning BMW of Hans Stuck/Chris Amon at the end of the six hours.

At Spa, the Belgian Promoteam lost Roger Dubos when his Group 1 GTV ran into Hans-Pieter Joisten's BMW, which had got out of control while lapping him, and the two cars cannoned off the Armco into Ballot Lena's Autodelta GTV. Tragically, both Dubos and Joisten were killed. A little later, Massimo Larini was badly injured when his GTAm went over a barrier and dropped down into a field. The team prize must have seemed small consolation to Promoteam.

To call a car 'old' when it is but three years out of the box, so to speak, may seem a little odd to those of us who have run classic cars as everyday transport. But that's how it was seen, and in racing terms, a great deal of development takes place in the course of one season, let alone three, so the GTAm's ability to stay on the pace in 1973 is all the more remarkable. This was the year of the Alfetta saloon's debut, at Mantorp Park, Sweden, complete with four-valve 256bhp 2-litre engine, and with the

unfamiliar driver pairing of F1 racers Rolf Stommelen/ Reine Wisell. After a good showing, the Alfetta retired with a dud clutch.

The Alfetta was back again for the Zandvoort 4 Hours with Stommelen/ Facetti driving, and there were two GTAms for Dini/Walter Dona and Zeccoli/Hans Deen. The Alfas were up against the 16-valve BMW 2002 of Kelleners/Menzel and several Escort RSs, with the Toyota Celicas now challenging. The Alfetta saloon had bigger brakes and clutch, but suffered from oil surge in the race, and retired whilst running 11th. The GTAms finished eighth and ninth, behind the works Capris and BMWs'

titanic struggle, and running with total reliability, despite pressure from the Celica.

At the Paul Ricard 6-Hours, the Alfa challenge rested on the GTAms, for there were some parts which had not arrived for the Alfetta. Facetti/Dini were on the sixth row of the 3 x 3 grid, with Zeccoli/Dona a row behind. Up front were all the aces like Amon/Stuck, Pescarolo/Wollek, Quester/Hezemans and Ickx/Hunt in 3.5 BMW CSLs, and Stewart/Mass, Larousse/Fitzpatrick in 3.0 Capri RSs, with an assortment of 2.0 Escort RSs separating them from the Alfas. Sadly, they didn't hold together, for Zeccoli's car's engine blew up at just over half distance, and Facetti's went

the same way, although the car had covered enough distance to be classified as a finisher.

The 1973 series drew to a close with the Tourist Trophy at Silverstone, and again there was no sign of the Alfetta, due, it was said, to strikes. The three GTAms of Facetti, Dini and Dona had their work cut out by now; Facetti kept going as fast as he could behind the Escorts, but Dini and Dona had terrible misfires from the outset. The race was a two heat affair, and since no engine changes were permitted between heats, the two sick GTAms had to soldier on as before. In the end, Facetti finished a creditable sixth overall, the winners being Derek Bell/Harald Ertl in an Alpina BMW, after a sterling drive by Jochen Mass in a Capri RS. The Escorts were sufficiently numerous, fast, and reliable to pip Alfa Romeo for the 2-litre class in the Championship by just one point.

However, it was not so much the advent of the new Alfetta saloon - the handling of which impressed everyone - which spelt the end for the GTA's competition career, but bureaucracy. In an extraordinary bout of rule-changing for the 1973 season, the under-1300cc class was axed, at a stroke eliminating the GTA Juniors from competing. One or two circuits included up-to-1300 categories in their Championship rounds, so there were a few privately entered GTA Juniors still about. Ford had just had its 1300cc BDA engine homologated, and the potential for some exciting duelling was lost. Not unnaturally, Carlo Chiti still believes the GTA 1300 Junior would have beaten the Escort 1300 BDA.

The 1973 results for Giulia Coupés and Berlinas were still good, especially in Italy and Germany, although not so numerous and far-flung as was once the case. The year began with Gerard Larrousse/Christian Delferrier (2000 GTV) winning the Group 1 class of the Monte Carlo Rally, and in July John Handley/John Clegg won the 2-litre class in the Tour of Britain. Meanwhile, back on the tracks Division 1 of the Monza 4-Hours was won by Regvart/Lang (GTAm), Facetti/Dini (GTAm) took Division 1 in the Nürburgring Touring Car Grand Prix and Dieter Meyer (GTA 1300 Junior) won the 1300 class. Imbert/Bijttebier (2000 GTV) took the Group 1 2-litre class in the Spa 24-Hours and Alfa Romeo won the Kings Cup. Bjorn Steenberg (GTA 1300 Junior) topped the podium at Mantorp Park whilst, down under, the Bathurst 1000kms was won by Ray Harrison/Malcolm Robertson (2000 GTV).

In 1974 GTV 2000s took the Kings Cup at Spa and Claude Ballot-Lena/Bernard Beguin won Division 3. The Vincent Delaval 2000 GTV was Group 1 winner in the Tour de France Automobile. Dieter Meyer (GTA 1300 Junior) won the 1300 Group 2 category in the Nürburgring 300kms, whilst Donato/Donato (GTAm) won the 2-litre Group 2 class in the Targa Florio. In Holland Hans Deen (2000 GTV) was the man to beat whilst in Poland Lattari (2000 GTV) was most successful. In Portugal Domingos and Bernardo Sa Nogueira continued to win everything in sight. The Dakar 6-Hours was won by Facetti/Demoulin (GTAm).

Whilst the 33/TT 12 sports prototypes were cleaning up in the World

Championship for Makes in 1975, the 2000 GTVs were still to the fore in Touring Car racing. Guy Frequelin (GTV 2000) was first in Group 1 on the Monte Carlo Rally and Bernard Beguin (2000 GTV) was home first in the Tour de France. At the Spa Francorchamps 500kms in May Andruet/Dini (2000 GTV) won Division 3 and Noé/De Deyne (GT 1600 Junior) took Division 2. Two months later the same car and driver pairing of Andruet/Dini won Division 2 in the Spa 24-Hours. Like most Italian events still, the Monza 4-Hours continued to be won by a Giulia Coupé; in this case the Chiapparini/Francia GT Sprint Veloce took the 1600 Group 2 class. The Monza 500 miles Touring Car race Division 3 was won by Finotto/Colzani (2000 GTV). Leo Bertorelli/Peter Hilliard (GT 1300 Junior) won Group 1 category in the Silverstone Tourist Trophy and Eddy Labinjoh (2000 GTV) cleaned up thoroughly north of the border.

By 1976 the Alfetta GTVs were victorious in the 2-litre Division 2 class and Spartaco Dini was European Champion, having been in the winning partnership in every round of the series. The Alfasuds were beginning to make their mark in the small capacity class but GTA 1300 Juniors were remarkably successful still. In Division 1 of the European Championship Chapparini/Premoli scooped the Monza 4-Hours and Tali/Dal Pozzo won at Mugello. At the Silverstone Tourist Trophy Vanoli/Hadorn came first in class, Mayer/Arend took the Nürburgring Grand Prix and 'Orfeo'/Braga won the Vallelunga 500kms.

90

Other major success included the Nürburgring 18-Hours, where Peter Uhrmacher (GT 1300 Junior) won the Group 1 1300 class. Beguin/Fauchille (2000 GTV) took the Group 1 honours in the 44th Monte Carlo Rally and Donato/Donato (GTAm) won the 2-litre Group 2 class in the 60th Targa Florio.

Whilst the Tipo 33/TT 12s enjoyed a walkover in the World Championship for Makes in 1977, the Giulia Coupés had just about reached the end of the line as far as major national and international races were concerned. They only managed one win in the European Touring Car Championship, the good old Monza 4-Hours, with

Chiapparini/'Gimax' (GTA 1300 Junior) collecting the laurels in Division 1. All other Alfa successes were down to Alfettas, Alfetta GTVs, Alfasuds and Alfasud Sprints, apart from the Zandvoort 4-Hours where Fornera/Franz (2000 GTV) won Division 3.

Rally Record

The GTA never made a significant showing in rallying, although there were a few private entrants. The big-name rallies like the Monte and the Alpine usually brought out well supported factory entries to steamroller private entrants, but Jean Rolland and Gabriel Augias did take the tough Coupé des Alpes in a GTA in

the 1966 Alpine Rally, in the process beating Roger Clark/Brian Melia's Lotus Cortina and Aaltonen/Liddon's Cooper S. The Frenchmens' GTA was fitted with a Conrero-built engine good for 140bhp. The same driver/car combination was to the fore in the Lyon-Charbonnieres rally in March 1967, going hard against Vic Elford/David Stone's Porsche 911, until the GTA broke its rear axle on one of the climbs. Other Jolly Club-run GTA pairings to feature quite well in rally results were Cavallari/Salvay, Hanrioud/Peray, Labaune/'Finkel' and Ramu-Caccia/Mauris. In the 1967 Alpine Rally the Alfa Romeo-France GTAs of Rolland, Jean-Claude Gamet, Henri Greder,

Below: The 2000 GTV of Guy Chasseuil/Christian Baron in a magnificent slide on the Col de Torini during the 1972 Monte Carlo Rally.

and '50s star Bernard Consten could not match Gerard Larrousse in the prototype 1600 Alpine-Renault A110. Although Consten, in a fine comeback, eventually ended up in second place overall, ten minutes behind Hopkirk/ Crellin's Cooper S and closely followed by the Gamets in another GTA.

Left: Mike Doughty's 1750 GTV raises the dust during the East African Safari Rally.

Below: The 1973 Monte Carlo Rally and the second placeAlfa 2000 GTV of Jean-Claude Lagniez/Martine Renier takes a hairpin at Peille.

For the 1968 Alpine Rally four Autodelta cars were prepared and run by the Paris Alfa dealer for Bernard Consten/Jean Todt, Jean-Claud and Michel Gamet, Guy Verrier/Francis Murac and Jean-Louis Barailler/Jean-Phillipe Fayel. Their ace was the Michelin-developed racing tyre, first tried the previous year in Corsica and providing for the Alfas far superior wet road traction to that obtained by the Fords and Alpines. As expected, the GTAs were quick on the road sections, frequently beating the Alpine-Renault and Lancia Fulvia times. The brothers Gamet even led the rally until their retirement at half-distance. Eventually Barailler took second place behind Vinatier's Alpine, but Alfa Romeo won the constructor's cup, helped by Lucien Bianchi bringing in his 1750 Berlina seventh.

Bianchi finished second, this time GTA-mounted, with Gamet third, in the 1968 Tour de Corse, regarded as the quickest of the international rallies. It was also one of the most dangerous with precipitous roadside drops into pine woods or the sea. Again, the winner was an Alpine-Renault A110 driven by Jean-Claude Andruet, but to finish at all was something when all the Porsches and most of the Lancias had retired.

The Nick Koob/Kridel GTA won the Amateur Trophy and its class in the 1968 Tulip Rally, which included a test on the Zolder circuit.

In the 1969 Alpine Rally, the 'works' Alfa Romeo challenge fizzled out early on when Wollek's time card was lost on a special stage and another two GTAs expired; the GTA of Barra/Payel won the 1300-1600cc class, which made up for an otherwise disappointing showing.

In rallying terms the general impression of the Alfa GTAs was that they were the quickest Group 2 Touring Cars on the road sections, certainly in 1966 and frequently in 1967 and again in 1968, but over the rough stages of rallies, the alloy-panelled cars were too fragile. It was thought at the time that Autodelta's general policy of hiring mostly Italian drivers placed the team at something of a disadvantage, when most of the rally aces came from northern Europe. Moreover, the factory-backed operations of Alpine-Renault, Ford Escort TC and Lancia Fulvia were just beginning to make themselves felt and, as always, Alfa Romeo's efforts were concentrated on the race circuit.

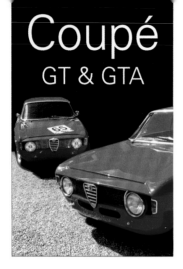

Coupé
GT & GTA

5

Recapturing
the Coupé

Bustling suburban Purley in Surrey is where you'll find the workshops of Alfa Romeo restoration expert Mike Spenceley and his small team of restorers. I first met Mike in the early 1990s at a UK National Alfa Day at Stanford Hall in Leicestershire, and we collaborated on the restoration chapters of two of my books, on Alfa Romeo Spiders and Alfa Romeo Berlinas (Sedans). Mike had already built up a strong reputation in the field and was emerging as the leading light on the reclamation of these cars. So, when my publisher Rod Grainger asked me to update this book, I naturally turned to Mike again, in view of the sad loss of Malcolm Morris who was our guide in the restoration chapter in the book's first edition.

Restoration expert
Mike Spenceley's business, MGS Coachworks, was set up in 1990 and was originally housed in a small two-car workshop in Caterham. He was a one-man-band in those days, restoring mostly classic Alfa Romeos, and listed Bell and Colvill as one of his regular clients. In 1996 MGS moved to its present location in Purley, on the edge of London, on what was previously Bell and Colvill's original site. A low bake oven was installed, and Mike recruited time-served craftsmen as his staff. Apart from the undoubted quality of workmanship, he attributes much of the firm's success to 'using only the best products and doing all our jobs correctly'.

Mike Spenceley's love of cars goes back to his childhood. 'I left school aged fifteen, to pursue my passion,' he said, 'and I served an apprenticeship in the paint trade. It was tough because the older guys really didn't want to share their knowledge beyond allowing me to rub down and prepare surfaces.' Nevertheless, he spent every spare minute practising on whatever came along and whenever he was allowed to. 'I remember a Mk 10 Jaguar as an episode of bleeding fingers and hurt

Restoration expert Mike Spenceley at his Purley workshops with the finished product - a 1750 GTV rescued from the brink. Prior to commencing a job, Mike discusses the customer's objectives for the car and advises accordingly. Courtesy Mike Spenceley

Right: Some dealers and restorers get involved with the competition side; Pieor Pesaro and a much modified Junior Zagato at Mallory Park in 1990.

Middle: A Junior Zagato for sale at Huntsworth Garage in 1990. The Junior Z had full-width plexiglass front and the tailgate could be opened for ventilation whilst the car was in motion.

pride,' he mused. It was clear from the outset that coachwork renovation was a process of constant learning, and Mike recalls ruefully that in the transition from old-fashioned cellulose to modern paint systems many older craftsmen were left behind. He went on to work for restorers specialising in Rolls Royce, Aston Martin, Porsche, BMW and Jaguar and, bearing in mind the levels of quality demanded by such machinery, he naturally became extremely proficient. By the late 1990s, Mike was being asked to judge the concours entries at the UK Alfa Romeo Owners' Club's National Alfa Day.

It's no accident that MGS Coachworks is renowned for its Alfa Romeo restorations. Mike Spenceley: 'My love of Alfa Romeos goes way back. I've always admired these cars. I've driven virtually every marque at some point in my life but, for me, there's no other car that offers such a comprehensive package of looks, performance and handling, even compared with the most expensive cars.' As well as restoring customer's Bertone GTs and saloons, MGS rebuilds cars for sale, and this is an excellent way of obtaining a first class example of the marque.

Project management

Before starting on a restoration Mike provides the vital guidance to his customers, assessing what the project will entail, how long it will take and

Paul O'Hanlon in a Huntsworth-prepared car during an Alfa Owners Club Autotest.

what it will cost. Mike is not alone in lamenting the fact that people expect to buy classic Alfas for the cost of a secondhand Ford Escort, and having them restored for similarly small sums of money. In 2002, fewer British customers could afford the price of a top class restoration, and Mike was attracting owners of restoration projects from abroad. He was philosophical, reasoning that although fewer restorations were actually going through, those that were being done resulted in better cars at the end of the day. He was also counselling patience to some of his clients, finding that some owners were looking for a quick fix.

The likely monetary value of the finished product, its sentimental value, and the pros and cons of doing it in the first place are crucial questions to be addressed, as are the issues of whether a part restoration or holding action is worth contemplating. With all the cars in the 105-Series Giulia range now over twenty-five years of age, only those from 'dry states' in the USA or perhaps South Africa will be free from corrosion. But Mike Spenceley exudes confidence. 'Our craftsmen are among the finest in the business, and we can fabricate any unavailable panel to the highest standard. Nothing is beyond our capabilities.' MGS will tackle anything from small repairs and scratches to a full-blown insurance claim. 'We apply strict attention to detail, and our colour matching on classic cars is first class. We can also carry out trim renovation, whether it is a full re-trim or a minor repair. We can also fit a new hood to a Spider or re-cover a sunroof to any requirement.' His mechanics are factory trained in Alfa Romeo and Ferrari marques, and can do engine and suspension rebuilds or simply carry out a full service.

Vulnerable aspects

Mike talked me through the vulnerable areas of the Bertone coupés. A lot of these points are perhaps obvious, and some corrosion issues are common to many classic cars. 'Let's start with the boot (trunk). Lift the lid up and look inside the boot, remove the spare wheel and check the well,' said Mike. 'Water can sit in there and rot it from the inside, while stones can damage it so it gets attacked from underneath as well. If it's rotted out it's best to cut it out. New wells are available and are not difficult to fit. Also, take a look around the petrol tank. This is a bit more difficult to repair but not impossible. It's important to make sure of a good seal as water can get in and cause corrosion. New petrol tanks for the coupés are becoming more difficult to find now, but it is possible to convert a Spider tank to fit. If we look at the leading edges of the boot-lid, you'll see how these can corrode. Boot-lids always rot along the trailing edge, and usually along the sides and around the hinges. A lot of condensation accumulates around the rear screens leading ultimately to corrosion. Rust around the rear shock absorber turrets is also a problem.'

Restorations usually begin with the sills, since the chassis derives much of its strength from these areas. 'Lift the front carpets and check the condition of the sills from the inside, and the front foot-wells as well,' said Mike. 'Take a look at the inner sill, particularly to the front of the car. It's probable that repairs have been carried out already, or will need doing. Have a look at the outer sills, the bottom of the wings adjacent to the sills, and take time to study all four jacking points. All these panels are available as repair sections, but bear in mind it would be costly to replace them all. However, it's worth considering that with modern paints and rust protection - and a quality repair job - you shouldn't have to do the job again.'

'Next, we'll have a look at the window surrounds, particularly below the rear screen. If this is badly corroded, we need to remove the rear screen and replace the complete panel (happily, this is still available). Some corrosion can also occur around the rear side glass, but again, repair sections are available for these areas. Doors can corrode badly along the bottoms and edges, but complete outer skins are available. There's also a repair section available for the lower inside door frame. Check the bottom of the front windscreen A-pillars. This can be tricky to repair if very bad.'

'With the car on a jack or axle stands, we need to examine the underneath, starting with the front panel. It's particularly vulnerable around the indicators and the panel's bottom edge. Lie on your back and look at the front crossmember where the anti-roll bar mounts are located. This is a common area of corrosion, and replacing the crossmember correctly means removing the front panel and radiator. Front panels and crossmembers are readily available, so an excellent repair is possible. We put plenty of protection around the crossmember when we've finished.'

'Rear wheelarches are another problem area in these cars,' said Mike. 'Again, you'll find good repair panels are available, including complete inner arches. I would recommend you replace the complete wing if the inner and outer arch and wing lowers are corroded. Replacing the inner is actually far easier once the outer wing has been removed. We always paint the inner arches with a rust inhibiting primer before fitting the outer wing. It's a good idea to paint as much of the inside as possible with good primers while you've got access.'

'Check the lower parts of all four wings,' Mike advised. 'It'll be immediately evident if there's paintwork blistering and signs of brown stains weeping out tells you it's rotten. If you're replacing the sills you'll replace the panels adjacent to the sills anyway. These are readily available. Have a look below the rear bumper at the bottom of the wings and rear valance. A complete rear panel is available and there are sections for the rear wings as well. There's also a lower rear valance available if you don't need to replace all of the rear panel.

Front wings can be saved by cutting out rotten metal at the bottom and incorporating repair sections that include the shape of the rolled edge of the wheelarch.

Strip down

Assuming that it's to be a full restoration, and not simply a localised accident damage repair or a cosmetic exercise, the restorer's first task is to remove all trim and seating from the car and, more than likely, strip out brake lines and the wiring loom. First to go are the external pieces, the bumpers, radiator grille, lights, hubcaps, followed by the doors and window glass, bonnet and boot-lid. Everything has to be labelled and identified to ensure nothing goes missing during the project. One exception may be the dashboard, which in the event the loom stays in, can be masked up to avoid disturbing the electrics. But this is to assume there's no rust present in the scuttle behind it. It's all according to the nature of the job whether it stays put or not. As Mike Spenceley points out, 'no-

one makes replacement dashboards, and it's difficult to source a good secondhand one. So, when checking out a prospective car, best be sure that the dashboard is in reasonable condition, even if the rest of the car needs attention.'

Once stripped out, the vehicle is likely to spend the next few months on axle stands, and the wheels will probably be sent off for shot-blasting before being resprayed. In the event that the car has to be moved around the workshop in the meantime, a set of mule wheels can be fitted.

Dents can be beaten out, and the area made good by careful filling and re-profiling. But corrosion is another matter, and the next question to be

When embarking on a restoration project, the car is totally stripped down. The first metal to go is the outer sill section, from the back of the front wheelarch to the front of the rear wheelarch. (Courtesy Mike Spenceley)

addressed is whether to cut out and apply patches or, more comprehensively, go for new panels. For example, if the spare wheel well only has a small hole in it, the easiest solution is to cut out the rotten area around the hole and weld in a metal patch. But if it is completely perforated with rot, the whole section ought to be cut out and a new panel welded in. The skilled restorer can construct repair patches with contours corresponding to the original section he's replacing. But it's often quicker and easier to fit a replacement wing than it is to cut out small sections of it and replace them with myriad patches.

Replacement panels are readily available from a small number of specialists. Among the better-known firms is Chris Sweetapple's Highwood Motor Company, which has been in operation in this field for at least a decade, and the long-running Westbury-based 'Italian Connection'. E.B. Spares supplies parts and panels for virtually all classic Alfa Romeos. The most recent arrival on the UK scene is Alfaholics, run by time-served Alfisti Richard Norris and Richard Banks.

Structural integrity

The 105-Series cars have unit-construction chassis/bodyshells and derive a great deal of their structural integrity from the sills. Mike Spenceley starts off his restoration of the Bertone Coupé by removing the outer sill section, which runs from the back of the front wheelarch to the front of the rear wheelarch, conforming to the area immediately below the doors. He also removes the lower wing sections front and rear, where they

Lower wing sections front and rear are also removed to access the inner sill. Typically, these internal panels need attention in any case. Depending on condition, the inner sill will either be replaced or repaired. (Courtesy Mike Spenceley)

The Giulia coupé sills are composed of inner, middle and outer sections and provide much of the rigidity of the unit-construction chassis. Here, the inner sill has been replaced and primed prior to installation of the middle and outer sections. (Courtesy Mike Spenceley)

100

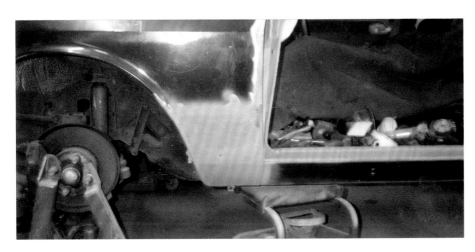

The outer sill and lower front wing section have been replaced using readily available repair panels. (Courtesy Mike Spenceley)

butt up to the sills, in order to access the inner sill. Having taken those areas away, he can get at the leading and trailing edges of the inner sill. It may be that the internal panels under the wings are in need of remedial action anyway, since they are in the direct line of fire for mud collection. Depending on condition, the inner sill is either replaced or repaired. Having got as far as accessing it, complete replacement seems the sensible course of treatment here.

When it's time for re-assembly, Mike administers copious amounts of anti-corrosive paint before replacing the outer sill panel. This is a type of pigment that's commonly used for painting steel bridges, and it contains zinc, a metal that isn't destroyed by heat when the outer sill - or any other inner panel - is welded on. The lower section of the front wing that was removed in order to perform the operation is refitted

and, since this is available as a repair panel, it makes sense to put a new bit on. The inner wheelarch panels that carry the suspension pick-up points may be perforated in places, and may withstand patching, which is less of a chore than cutting them out to make way for a whole new replacement. Generally, outer panels are much easier to replace than inner ones.

When the Coupés weren't worth a lot of money, owners just kept them on the road and got them through legal roadworthiness checks as best they could because they were such fun to drive. Now, in a financial sense the cars are worth looking after properly. But first Mike has to get rid of all the bodging of the past and get back to solid metal. A popular dodge with the Coupé sill section was to patch round the outside with metal foil, then cover that with fibreglass filler, smother it with bitumen

and finally paint it to match the body colour. No attempt was made to address the real problem of disintegrating metal. When rebuilding sills, some restorers box the whole section off so no damp can get into it, before putting the wings on and seam-welding right down the recess, rather than simply relying on spot welds. However, Mike believes the best course of action is actually to paint the sill components properly, and then the whole area should be secure.

The jacking points are particularly vulnerable on Bertone Coupés. After cutting out the rotten sections, new metal is welded in, restoring the strength to the side of the car. Then the sill panel is replaced and the restorer can start progressing towards the back and front of the car, working over the inner wheelarches, before replacing the outer wing panels (fenders) with new ones. It's crucial to get the strength back in the sills and the jacking points.

Spare wheel wells normally have rubber bungs which can be removed for drainage, but when the spare is in place you can't see the water in the well bottom and this is a typical breeding ground for rust. There are two huge rubber grommets in the car's front floorpan, two in the rear floorpan, two under the rear seat and another two in the spare wheel well. It's possible to get a rough idea of what the floor condition is like simply by turning up the carpet edges. If the signs are bad, the seats will have to come out so the carpet can be removed completely.

The most difficult part of the Coupé's body to restore used to be the area around the bottom of the rear

Boot floors are vulnerable to moisture inside - especially in the spare wheel well - and stone chips underneath. Corrosion levels are about typical here, but can be much worse. (Courtesy Mike Spenceley)

The spare wheel well has been completely replaced and the boot floor patched. (Courtesy Mike Spenceley)

screen, from one back wing to the other, because it had to be remade a bit at a time, by cutting a section of rotten metal out and making up a new portion and welding it in. That was time consuming and difficult because of all the complex shapes in that area of the car. But, happily, there is a repair section available for the whole area now.

Rear wings tend to corode beneath the rear bumper and all round the wheelarches. Rust tends to begin around the lip of the arch itself, where moisture has seeped between the two skins (these are simply folded over and create a convenient ledge on which mud accumulates). Another key area for rot is underneath the back of the rear quarter panel.

Door skins aren't difficult to get hold of these days, but they do take time to fit. If it's just a matter of a dent, it can be beaten out. Coupé doors rot around the handle because originally there was no gasket between the handle and the door skin. Now, though, a gasket is available, and MGS Coachworks will fit them during a restoration. Every time the door is opened, the handle rubs against the paintwork and eventually chips it away so that the door rots. When closing a Coupé door you should close it with a hefty swing, with your hand flat on the handle. Doors are particularly difficult to shut when new rubber door seals have been fitted.

Doors also rot because drain holes get blocked. Drainage is fundamental to the survival of door bottoms since, if the drain holes do get blocked, there's nowhere for rainwater and condensation to go. Panels received only a thin film of black undercoat on the inside when the cars were built, so they were poorly protected and vulnerable to corrosion from the start. The other place to examine is on the top edge of the door, along the moulding. Water gets under the trim and starts corrosion. Window channels are now available in aluminium, which addresses that potential rust problem.

The front wing tends to go along the bottom edge, at the rear. Mud gets trapped here and, even if there is a splash guard inside the wheelarch, moisture will still seep behind it. The splash or stone guards also cause problems because they rub against the metal, erode any sealer and the rust sets in. Stone chips on the edge of the wings also start rust. Splash or stone guards are available in fibreglass or aluminium now.

Water can get trapped in the valance underneath the radiator and will set off corrosion there; it can start rotting out the crossmember underneath the radiator as well. If it takes hold round the anti-roll bar mounting points it will affect the handling of the car. The front panel comprises the area in front of the bonnet, includes the headlight and grille area, and meets with the wings and the valance. Care is needed with the 2000 GTV and later 1600 GT Junior grilles because they are cast zinc alloy and are easy to break. They are available these days, so it's not necessary to substitute a chrome or stainless steel Alfa shield, as used to be the case. The difference between the 1750 and 2000 front panel is that there's a little bracket which

The section under the rear screen and the C-pillar can now be replaced with a repair panel - it used to be the most difficult part of the Bertone shell to repair. (Courtesy Mike Spenceley)

Right: Hidden behind the bumper, the rear panel and valance have rotted along the line of the boot floor.

Radical, but shows what can be involved if you're serious about restoring a coupé.

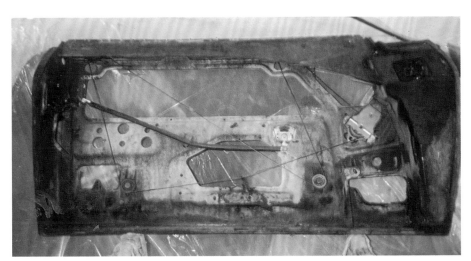

Looking like something unearthed from an archaeological dig, this is in fact a doorframe after the outer skin has been removed. (Courtesy Mike Spenceley)

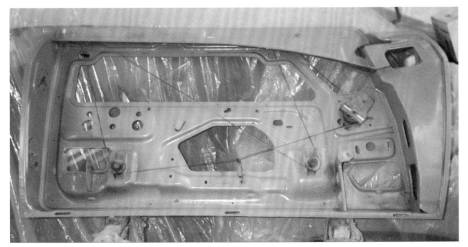

Here's that door frame again, after shot-blasting, repairs and a coat of primer. The next job is fitting a new outer skin. (Courtesy Mike Spenceley)

holds the 1750 centre grille on. All the fixings are the same, so the mesh grilles could be inserted each side. In the early days of replacement panels, it was possible to buy a front panel and a pair of front wings as one unit, but the practice stopped because crating and shipping such a large object was too expensive.

Bonnets usually remain intact because they are kept warm by the engine, and also because they have a fine patina of oil on them from the engine. The scuttle panel often corrodes, though. Because it's meant to come out, you'll find that it's loose, so there's always a bit of movement there which tends to chip the paint off.

There are a number of small idiosyncrasies with these cars which to be taken into account. For example, the Mark 1 1750 GTV had the sidelights in the bumpers, whereas the Mark 2 had them on the front panel, which is why there is a hole underneath the sidelight of later front panels. It was fitted with a rubber bung and the wires came through to the light on the bumper, but Alfa Romeo never dispensed with the hole when the light was moved to the front panel.

Paint by numbers
The days of cellulose paint are, of course, long gone. Tough, resin-based two-pack paints have been the order of the day for the last 15 years. These require a different environmental regime, of course, and for the painter to be fully protected with an air-fed mask because of the isocyanate poisons in the pigment. They should also be used in a proper low-bake oven. All paints are of a lower solvent content nowadays, and body shops have to keep a stringent record of solvents used.

Looking up at the front panel, this picture shows rust in the crossmember. In this case it was only necessary to replace the lower section, although complete front valances are available. (Courtesy Mike Spenceley)

The front valance has repair section installed. MIG-weld is ground back and any imperfections filled before priming. (Courtesy Mike Spenceley)

Mike sprays his cars with two coats of etch primer, then a high-build primer is applied on top of the etch primer, and the two coats bond together. The surface is then flatted down and any imperfections made good. The car is re-primed with another two or three coats of primer, depending on the level of rectification that's taken place. If the car is being painted with a metallic paint, it's rubbed down with a finer wet and dry paper, whereas, if it's to be a solid colour it will be finished with a slightly coarser paper. This is because the metallic paint, which has a thinner consistency than solid colour paints, acts as a base coat and is then lacquered.

Three layers of two-pack colour coat are then applied, assuming, of course, that the car is to be finished in a solid hue. The thickness of these three coats is the equivalent of no less than 21 coats of cellulose. This might seem impressive, but it's actually a fallacy that more paint on the car is better, having more paint means that it can chip more easily. What's important is the way it's applied, and that's where the specialist painter excels.

To obtain a metallic finish, three colour coats are followed by two coats of lacquer. Pigments dry extremely quickly and, after something like eight minutes, another coat of paint or lacquer can be applied. The thickness of three layers of two-pack paint is the equivalent of over 20 coats of cellulose, something the cars would never have got at the factory, especially in the boot space.

When the painting operation is complete, all inner sections are injected

With the whole car in primer, the engine bay and boot (trunk) are painted separately so that the powertrain and ancillaries can be installed without risking damage to finished coachwork. (Courtesy Mike Spenceley)

film on the inner box sections and is, therefore, permanent.

It's more than likely that a full-blown restoration will require some new trim or upholstery. All items are available, from original fabric seat covers tand head-linings, to carpet sets and rubber mats for the GT Junior. The best sources in the UK are the Highwood Motor Company, EB Spares, Alfashop, or Alfaholics.

At MGS Coachworks, prior to trimming the interiors, the car floor is painted with a rust-inhibiting primer - 'just like they use on metal bridges,' said Mike Spenceley. All the old felt matting will have been thrown in the skip, and once the rust-inhibitor has been applied, new sound-deadening pads are heated up and 'melted' onto the floor pans. No more soggy felt! Then the whole floor area is painted in satin black, and then the carpets or rubber mat sets are fitted. Seats are reinstated, suitably trimmed, as are door panels, furniture, head-linings and the centre console. The restoration is virtually complete.

Component sourcing

The spare parts situation for Bertone Coupés is constantly improving, and in addition to several sources for re-manufactured and New Old Stock components there are two or three specialists which sell secondhand parts from broken cars. It's a sign of the times that your local Alfa dealer has little idea of the marque's heritage and probably won't recognise anything earlier than an Alfa 155 or 164, let alone 105-Series cars. There's little point in getting service and maintenance work done on one of these

The bodyshell is painted with up to six coats of primer and three coats of two-pack top coat - Dutch blue in this case. (Courtesy Mike Spenceley)

with cavity wax, which is the same material used in construction of modern Alfa Romeos, Fiats, VWs, etc. Waxoyl has become largely a thing of the past as far as restorers are concerned, because it runs when hot and will need to be re-applied. Cavity wax is the preferred choice nowadays since it dries to a

Closure panels - the doors, bonnet and boot-lid - are painted separately, and fitted once the body is ready. Then the lights, bumpers and trim are applied.

cars at anywhere other than a classic or long-standing Alfa specialist.

Among the spares specialists offering 105-Series bits in Europe, Afra in Milan is an independent company dealing in spares, but is part of the authorised dealer network and is also

The interior of this 1750 GTV Mk 1 looks stunning in non-standard leather - it added about £4K to the whole restoration. Trimming was carried out at MGS coachworks, but complete carpet and mat sets are available in original colours and materials, so any good trimmer can fit them. (Courtesy Mike Spenceley)

This newly restored 1600 GTA belongs to Bo Johnsson, boss of a Volvo workshop in Hallstahammar, Sweden. (Courtesy Robert Petersson)

the official retailer of competition parts. There's another company called Spitzer in Neubach, Germany, offering all the panels and panel sections. They even offer the Dunlop brake components for early cars. The Schumacher father-and-son partnership operating as Usarto on the outskirts of Rotterdam is also a key source for parts.

In California there is Alfa Ricambi, and Europarts Connection, both of which have comprehensive catalogues for Bertone parts. They even do brand new hubcaps – maybe they are re-manufactured, but they look and feel absolutely right.

In the UK, the former keeper of the 105-Series Giulia Register, Chris Sweetapple, is principal of the Highwood Motor Company and he holds a large stock of parts, virtually anything you might need, both new and used, for the Bertone Coupés and other 105-Series Alfas. Of particular interest is the range of re- manufactured panels and repair sections - certainly the largest selection in the UK. Closure panels like bonnet, boot and doors are available in aluminium, which is convenient if restoring or building a GTA replica.

Historically, the best-known spare parts supplier in the UK is EB Spares of Westbury, Wiltshire, while the Alfaholics concern set up recently by Richard Norris and Richard Banks is also a principal source. Jeremy Wales at Alfashop in Norwich is better known as an Alfetta and Alfasud specialist, but he can source 105-Series components in Italy. For 101- and 105-Series brake parts, Tony Stevens' Alfastop is the leading source.

Mechanical matters

Typical mechanical parts that regularly need replacing on Giulia Coupés include shock-absorbers, track-rod ends, kingpins and bushes, all of which have a limited life. Worthwhile suspension tweaks include lowering ride-height, resetting camber and fitting high quality dampers. Fitting a larger capacity engine from another model in the 105-Series range brings an instant gain in performance, and a TwinSpark unit from an Alfa 75 is

worth considering. Electrics can be a dodgy area, in particular the lighting circuit where bulbs often blow possibly due to poor earthing (grounding). Other possible weaknesses in the mechanical department include the bearings in the propshaft universal joints; if you hear a curious rumbling coming from below the car that's what it may be.

Mike Spenceley has a few words of advice for anyone going to view a Bertone Coupé. 'On the mechanical front, as for all 105-Series cars, warm the engine, check the oil pressure, and listen for timing chain rattle. The top chain can be adjusted easily but the bottom can't. Drive the car and check the gearbox for wear - it should be an easy gear change when warm. If it graunches from third to second, the synchro is worn. And check that it doesn't jump out of reverse gear. Check for noise from the back axle, and suspension creaks and groans. I do recommend that you take a knowledgeable mechanic with you when inspecting a car, or do plenty of reading up on Alfa 105 mechanicals,' says Mike. Best bet for gearbox overhauls and rebuilt gearboxes is Charlie Skinner's Cloverleaf Transmissions in West London. For engine rebuilds, I'd recommend Richard Drake in Norwich, from personal experience. He's done a number engines for Julius Thurgood's 105-Series race cars including Top Hat and GTA Challenge runners. Probably the top engine specialist in the Netherlands is Willem van Voorthuyzen, whose Duetto Tuning premises in Amsterdam is a veritable Alladin's cave of GTA engine parts. One of Toine Hezeman's mechanics in the 1970s,

Willem is a mine of information on GTA powertrains – he was instrumental in the discovery that fitting a 1300 head on a 1600 block gave more power - and owns the ex-Hezemans 1750 GT Am. Not only that, his wife drives a perfectly innocuous-looking 2000 GTV, which was owned by Willem's father and ran in the 1974 Spa 6-Hours race. Willem is such a 105-Series supremacist that he won't work on an Alfa made after 1974.

Cars built before 1967 require a particular gear lubricant, and that is Shell 'Dentax'. This is quite an important consideration as ordinary gear oil shortens the life of the synchromesh. From early-1967 onwards, the gearboxes got molybdenum synchro rings, and could be filled with an ordinary EP (extreme pressure) gear oil. Dentax is hard to get now, but a suitable alternative is Castrol ST 90.

It is not uncommon for pre-1967 cars to have seized lower front suspension-arm bushings. As the arms are fixed to the crossmember by two bolts each side, if the bushings seize the mountings can pull out of the crossmember. Later cars had different suspension arm bushings and the fixing was changed to four bolts per side. There is a tendency for Giulias to blow head gaskets, due to the aluminium block and steel wet-liners expanding at different rates when heating up. This allows oil under pressure to blow past the six O-ring seals between head and block. Whenever the cylinder is removed it is advisable to have it checked for warping and, if necessary, skimmed. With its all-aluminium engine, you

One of the top 105-Series engine specialists is Willem van Voorthuyzen who owns a couple of GTAs and rebuilds GTA engines at his Duetto Tuning business in Amsterdam, Holland. (Courtesy Mike Spenceley)

The restoration of 1600 GTA 613102 is almost complete, as Bo Johansson makes some of the final connections in the engine bay. (Courtesy Robert Petersson)

will be doing your Alfa a favour if you drive gently until the engine's normal operating temperature has been reached. It's a good idea, too, to make sure that the coolant includes a good quality corrosion inhibitor suitable for alloy engines.

The 105-Series engines are basically very reliable and long-lived. The smaller capacity units can, in the heat of the moment, be taken all the way to 7000rpm. In fact, they seem to like being driven hard and choke up with carbon if they spend too long in an urban environment. Sometimes owners put the wrong spark plugs in their Giulia engines and burn holes in the pistons. Whilst these engines are susceptible to piston holing - which can also be caused by an over-weak fuel mix - they are not as sensitive to plug choice as rumour has it.

Golden Lodge plugs were originally recommended to Alfa owners by Giulio Ramponi, and it was apparently he who created the myth that they were the only plugs you could run in an Alfa twin-cam engine. It is true that they nave been fitted as original equipment since the '50s, and Alfa Romeo still won't recommend anything else. However, today, some specialists will only use NGKs, which have the reputation of functioning well at all temperatures. Along with other people, I have raced with NGK plugs in a GTV6 with no ill effects. In fact, these plugs are said to cure other running problems too; whereas Golden Lodges will oil up, NGKs won't. If you want to play safe, fit Golden Lodges but, if you are experiencing oiling problems, try other high quality plug

Robert Petersson carried out a back-to-back test between his 2000 GT Am replica and a modern 3.0-litre 24-valve GTV for his magazine Auto Motor & Sport. The classic racer proved to be 20 percent quicker around Mantorp Park circuit. (Courtesy George Johansson)

The Alfa Romeo GTV in its 21st Century incarnation. Launched in 1995, the two-plus-two GTV was styled by Pininfarina and Fiat Centro Stile, and was eventually available with 2.0-litre TwinSpark and 3.0-litre 24-valve V6 engines driving through the front wheels. Unlike its Bertone forebears, this GTV left the racing side to its 156 touring car sibling. (Courtesy Alfa Romeo)

One you wouldn't mind dancing with. Liane Engemann rounds Paddock Bend at Brands Hatch, 1971, in the Team Radio Veronica GTA Junior. (Courtesy Ian Catt)

brands. Jon Dooley used Golden Lodge in his Ferraris because they produced a softer spark and better-distributed burn. He claimed Golden Lodges were only problematic if left in too long. Also speaking in favour of Golden Lodge, the Roger Clark Team established that they gave an increase of 4bhp over other comparable spark plugs in their Group 1 2000 GTVs.

Driving experience

If you drive a Bertone Coupé today, having spent the last twenty-five years driving more modern machinery, you'll find yourself pleasantly surprised. At first the car will seem gawky and light on its feet, which will be partly to do with the fact that it's likely to be running painfully thin-looking 165 x 14 Cinturatos. These are indeed much narrower and therefore more responsive than modern rubber. Probably the brakes will feel a little unresponsive, the steering light and, depending on your terms of reference, the gearchange slow, albeit wonderfully precise. If you happen to be transferring from an Alfetta or Alfa 75, you'll actually find the Giulia gear selection process swift and slick by

Robert Petersson guides his 1600 Sprint GT through the traffic on a Sunday afternoon outing. (Courtesy Ulla-Carin Ekblom)

comparison! There may be something odd about the pedals, too. That's because in all right-hand-drive and early left-hand-drive models the pedal box is floor-mounted, meaning the pedals pivot from the floor rather than using the pendant mounting style, which is pretty much normal practice now.

In these days of fuel-injection, most of us have forgotten about priming the carbs as you had to in your non fuel-injection Bertone Coupé. Four dabs on the accelerator pedal, turn the ignition key and she'd fire up without using the choke at all. You might have to work away at it a little bit to keep her going, of course, but that was all part of the machismo of running an Alfa! Paradoxically, you knew that because of the Coupé's all-alloy engine you weren't meant to rev it hard until it was thoroughly warmed up, but the temptation was always to do just that: to blast away, revelling in the rasping twin-cam exhaust note and the sucking of big carburettors. In fact, the recommendation was to let the engine idle for three minutes until it was good and warm. The stylish hand-throttle lever down below the dash was redundant really, because you couldn't rely on leaving the car with the hand-throttle set; the revs would creep up the warmer the engine got. To start the car when the engine's hot it's best to press your right foot to the floor and then wind it up. NGK plugs also facilitate hot starting.

Once under way, the car would feel taut and composed, its attitude always one of nose raised and tail down. She would rock nervously at traffic lights and, out on a fast secondary road, might feel inclined to be slightly wayward; like old-fashioned ballroom, you'd be dancing with her as she glided through the bends. You influenced her progress with the accelerator pedal and slick movements through the gearbox, of course, but trimmed her line with minute adjustments of accelerator: off, to make her nose tuck in; on lightly, to pull it out again. You could slide her if you wanted to by stepping on the gas and applying an appropriate amount of opposite lock: but had to be ready to catch her quick before she swapped ends. A club practice evening or track-day is just the place to indulge in this pastime, and a properly set-up Giulia is always a joy to chuck about for a few laps. But fit a spare set of wheels shod with well-worn tyres first, and call it a day when the brakes cry enough.

In normal road-going use there was never any problem about stopping your Giulia. My engine-swapping experience established that even a single-servo'd 1300 system was enough to retard a 2.0-litre-powered Giulia. The larger-engined cars had the benefit of dual-circuit twin servos as standard, of course. The transfer from Dunlop discs to Ate brakes in 1967 was a significant improvement.

Other traits? Avoid changing from third to second gear without double-de-clutching: your feet will be moving

Dice of the Day. The inaugural GTA Challenge at Donington in May 2002 produced an epic battle between the second and third placed cars of Mark Hales and James Diffey, as the motoring journalist held off the hard-charging historic racer to take second place.
(Courtesy Nicholas Froome, www.bolide.co.uk)

like Fred Astaire or Gene Kelly, but you'll avoid the graunch which damages the selectors. The 'knife-through-butter' gearshift was always regarded as the world's best in the '60s. There is more room inside the 105-Series Coupé than in the earlier 750- and 101-Series models and the average-sized motorist could feel comfortable enough, even if lanky northern European types could never quite hit it off with the 'Italian Ape' driving position. This expression simply meant that the relationship between the pedals and the steering wheel forced the driver to adopt a stretched-arm and bent-legged driving position behind the steering wheel. Cars fitted with the dished wood-rim steering wheel offered some improvement in driver comfort. But you do get used to the driving position and can distract yourself by savouring the car's other qualities, or stop for a break if it starts to get uncomfortable.

The Coupé's back seats are ideal only for children but, as with all two-plus-twos, a couple of adults will find a way to get squashed in, if necessary. Commenting on the accessibility of the 1750 GTV in *Motor Sport* in 1968,

This is the 1300 GTA Junior run by Turin-based Squadra Corse Monzeglio from 1969 to 1971, during which time Luigi Pozzo scored 20 wins, including the 1971 Italian Touring Car title. Between 1972 and 1975, the car was run by Swiss driver Rudi Franz. It was acquired by Siggi Brunn in 1996, and he ran it in the 1997 Tour de France retrospective. (Courtesy Nick Atkins, Gilford Motorsport)

Andrew Marriott said he found that, 'when stepping out of the car it was necessary to place a leg well outside to avoid scraping dirt from the door-ledge onto one's trouser leg; a funny complaint which must have something to do with the low-mounted seats and wide sill.'

There was never enough interior ventilation in the Giulia Coupés, although the 2000 GTV had eyeball vents each end of the dash. However,

back in the '60s people weren't afraid of the elements; you just opened the quarter-light windows.

In common with most of its contemporaries, and even the Alfetta generation, driving at night in the Giulia Coupé was not an entirely pleasurable experience. The Carello headlights provided reasonable illumination on high beam, but the transition to dip was disappointing, to put it mildly. One contemporary solution to this was to fit rally-spec 100-watt bulbs and bigger fuses if they blew.

Unless you are concerned to keep your Bertone Coupé utterly standard, these are some of the simple do-it-yourself modifications that will make your car a little more user-friendly in the '90s. Fit more powerful lights - or spotlamps. Install a set of aftermarket dampers - Konis are probably the best bet - with hard settings at the front and soft at the rear. A set of 185/70 x 14, or 195/60 x 14 tyres will improve grip tremendously without compromising the ride, but will take the edge off handling and 'feel' slightly. Fitting heavy boots instead of light pumps can make your dancing partner apt to tramline.

This is what it looks like when a GT Am fills your mirrors - Robert Petersson at Mantorp Park. (Courtesy George Johansson)

A trio of classic Alfa race cars at Knutstorp, Sweden, in 1999. The maroon Giulia Super (43) is that of Arne Allard, a leading Fiat-Abarth driver in the 1960s, who also owns a 1600 GTA formerly raced in the Swedish championship in the late 1960s by Harald Kronegård. At centre is an Autodelta-built GTA (46) belonging Bo Johnsson. The car was originally acquired from Carlo Chiti in 1967 by Kjell Ehrman and is (probably) chassis number 613162, and still has its Autodelta engine, no. AD 133. A consistent front runner in historics, Bo Johnsson has had the car since the early 1980s when it was in wide Modsports form. He was also the builder of the GT Am replica (no 38) belonging to Robert Petersson. (Courtesy Robert Petersson)

The Giulia Sprint GT - showing off her elegant profile in a contemporary press picture - to drive on today is to experience forgotten pleasures.

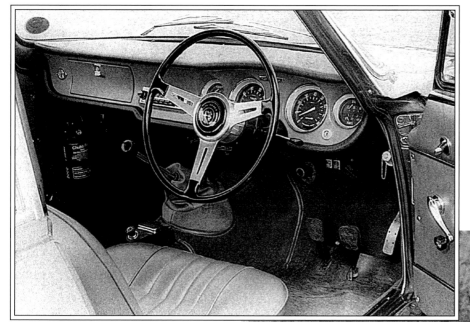

Bertone Coupés force drivers into the long arms, short legs driving position. Awkward floor-mounted clutch and brake pedals on many examples can compound the discomfort.

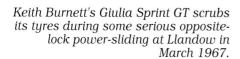

Keith Burnett's Giulia Sprint GT scrubs its tyres during some serious opposite-lock power-sliding at Llandow in March 1967.

Cutaway extolling the virtues of Alfa's 1750 GT Veloce from a contememporary sales brochure. The reference to "bent type" exhaust preventing backflow seems to have lost something in the translation from Italian ...

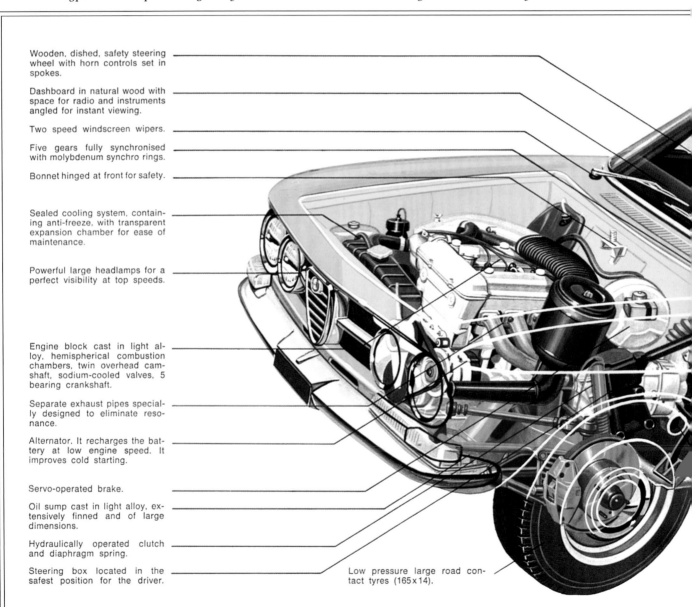

Wooden, dished, safety steering wheel with horn controls set in spokes.

Dashboard in natural wood with space for radio and instruments angled for instant viewing.

Two speed windscreen wipers.

Five gears fully synchronised with molybdenum synchro rings.

Bonnet hinged at front for safety.

Sealed cooling system, containing anti-freeze, with transparent expansion chamber for ease of maintenance.

Powerful large headlamps for a perfect visibility at top speeds.

Engine block cast in light alloy, hemispherical combustion chambers, twin overhead camshaft, sodium-cooled valves, 5 bearing crankshaft.

Separate exhaust pipes specially designed to eliminate resonance.

Alternator. It recharges the battery at low engine speed. It improves cold starting.

Servo-operated brake.

Oil sump cast in light alloy, extensively finned and of large dimensions.

Hydraulically operated clutch and diaphragm spring.

Steering box located in the safest position for the driver.

Low pressure large road contact tyres (165x14).

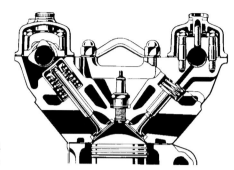

A cross-section of the Giulia's twin cam cylinder head.

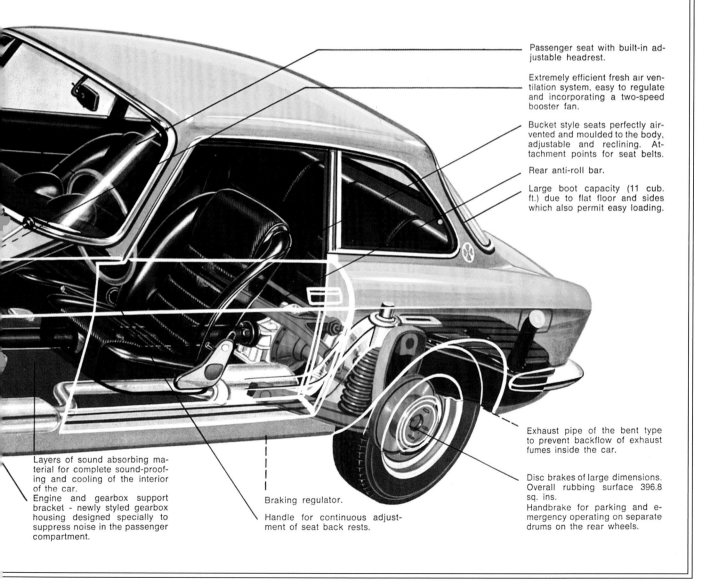

Passenger seat with built-in adjustable headrest.

Extremely efficient fresh air ventilation system, easy to regulate and incorporating a two-speed booster fan.

Bucket style seats perfectly airvented and moulded to the body, adjustable and reclining. Attachment points for seat belts.

Rear anti-roll bar.

Large boot capacity (11 cub. ft.) due to flat floor and sides which also permit easy loading.

Exhaust pipe of the bent type to prevent backflow of exhaust fumes inside the car.

Disc brakes of large dimensions. Overall rubbing surface 396.8 sq. ins.
Handbrake for parking and emergency operating on separate drums on the rear wheels.

Layers of sound absorbing material for complete sound-proofing and cooling of the interior of the car.
Engine and gearbox support bracket - newly styled gearbox housing designed specially to suppress noise in the passenger compartment.

Braking regulator.

Handle for continuous adjustment of seat back rests.

Cutaway view of Alfa's evergreen twin-cam engine, here in 2-litre form.

*These drawings show clearly the
component parts making up the
Coupé's sideframe, rear bulkhead
boot/trunk floor. If you're making
welded repairs, the structural
integrity of all these components has
to be restored.*

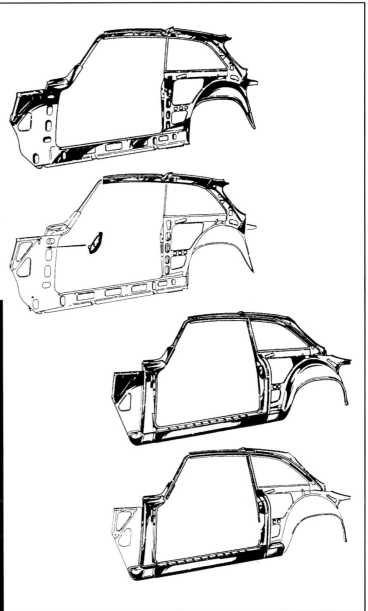

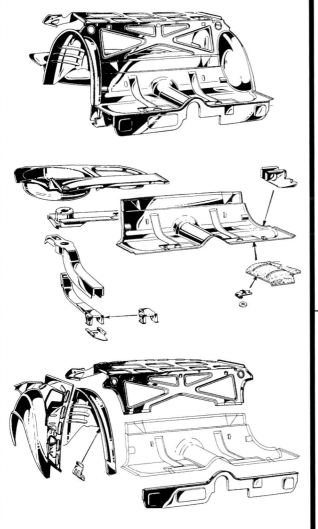

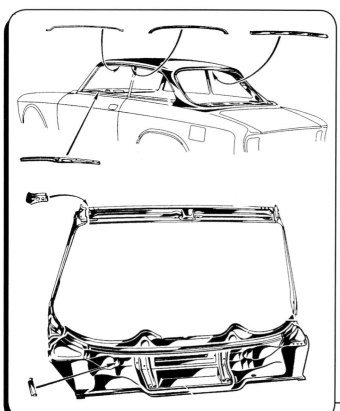

Left: The Coupé roof structure with strengthening cross braces. Also shown is the complex frame structure which supplies rigidity to the rear window aperture and the rear deck. If rust gets into this structure it's difficult to fix.

Below: The sideframe struiture of the rare Giulia GTC convertible. Reinforced sills/ rocker panels help to replace the torsional rigidity lost in the process of decapitation.

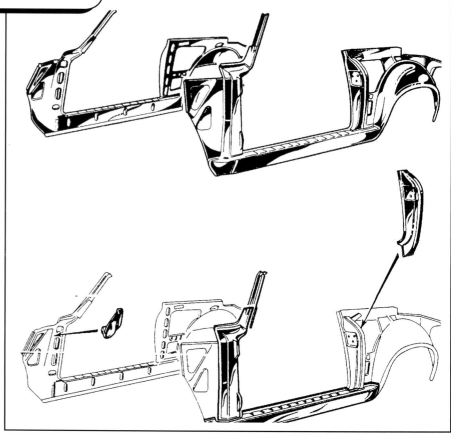

More structural details of the CTC showing panels and reinforcements unique to the model. Once again, it is essential that the integrity of all these components is restored during structural repairs.

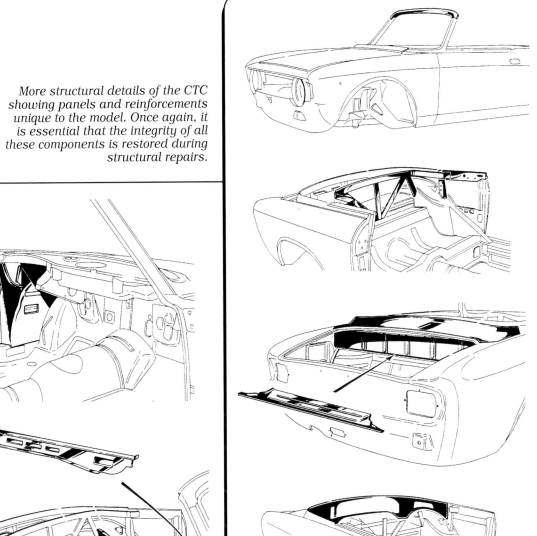

Every Giulia owner and restorer's dream! A parts department with floor to ceiling racks stretching into the distance and all packed full of pristine Alfa parts. Amongst 105-Series parts on view are boot floor moulding

at left, front bulkhead at centre and Super/TI doors at right. This page shows another section of same parts warehouse (note the half-front panel for a 2600 Spider). Both photos taken at Alfa GB, around 1969.

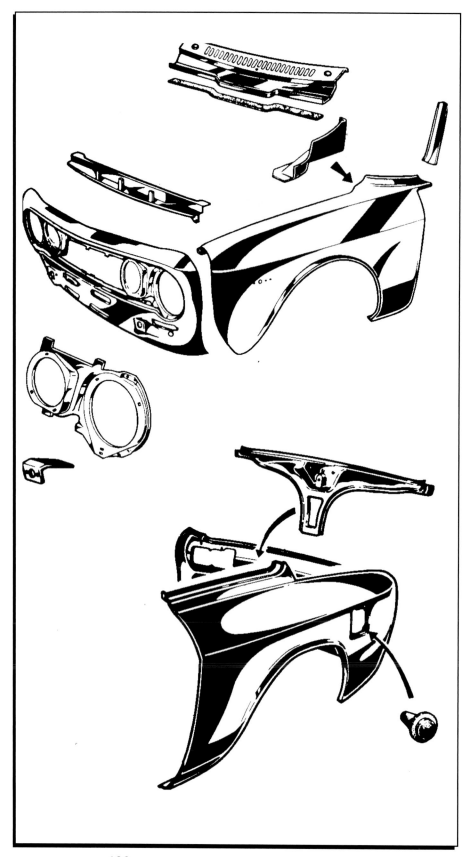

Left: The Giulia Coupé's major outer body panels. The quality of reproduction replacements can be variable and, even with the very best quality panels, a considerable amount of trial-and-error positioning will be necessary to achieve the best harmony between adjacent panels.

Right: The suspension system that gives the Giulia its sure-footed handling. Front suspension top, and rear below. Generally speaking if you want to achieve a really taut feel to a restored car, you'll need to renew all wearable parts such as bushes, bearings, ball joints and shock absorbers as cumulative wear in these components takes the edge off handling. New coil springs will restore original ride height. Both wheel types and all the wheel trims shown were available for the Coupé.

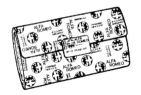

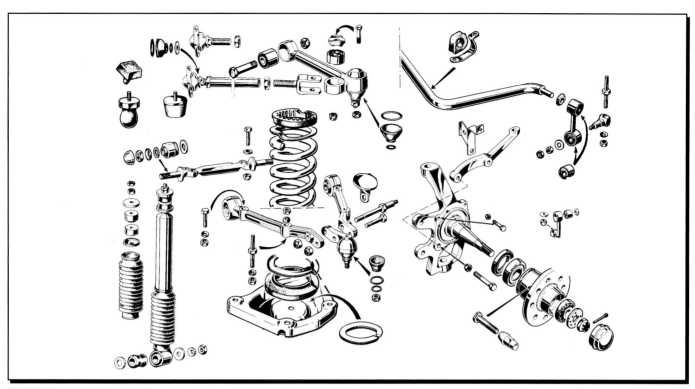

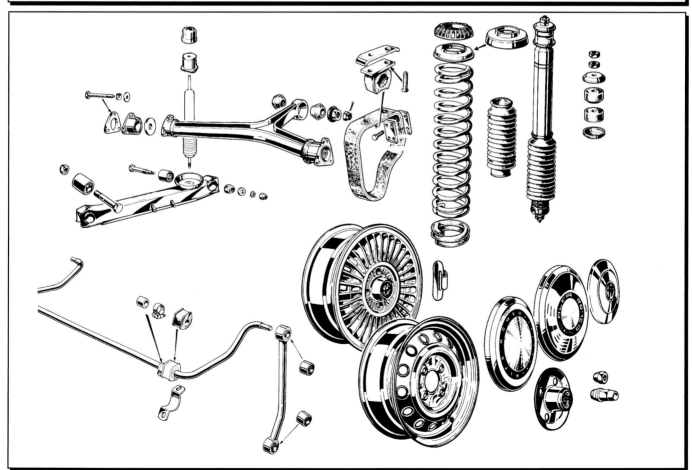

Top right: Components of the carburettor type fuel system, including tank - which commonly rusts around its seams - manifold, fuel pump and fuel filter. Pairs of Webers, Solexs or Dell'Ortos were fitted and all gave broadly similar performance, however Webers are generally favoured. This Parts Catalogue drawing also shows gasket and jet sets.

Below: Alfa's classic five-speed gearbox is a joy to use and was well ahead of its time when introduced. Common problems are worn synchro on 2nd gear and a tendency to jump out of reverse gear if the selector fork is worn or bent.

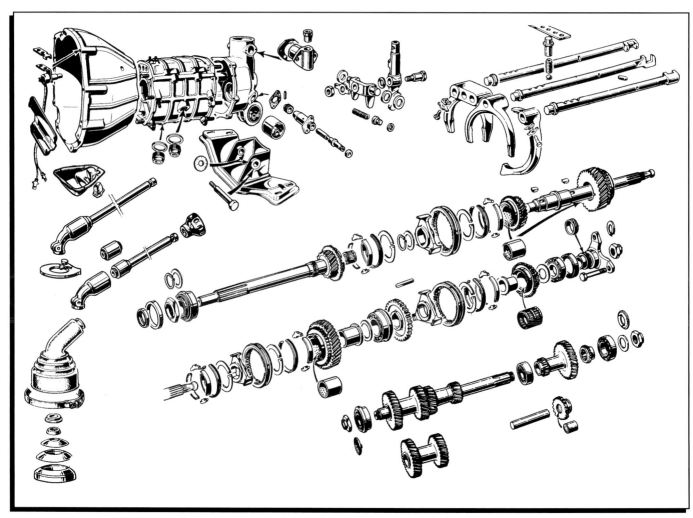

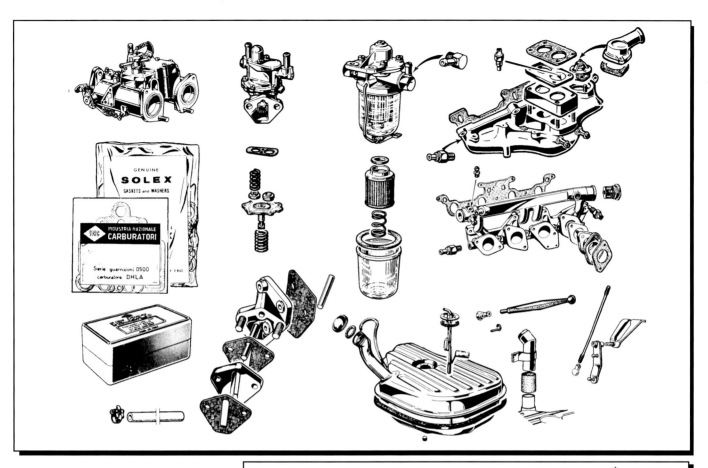

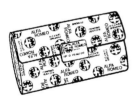

Right: Schematic of Spica fuel injection system as fitted to US-destined cars. Set up properly, the system can be good but inexeperienced tinkering and general wear can make it problematic.

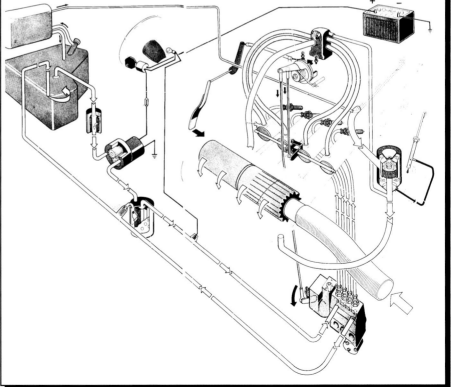

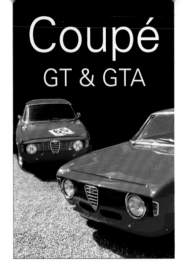

Coupé
GT & GTA

6

Classic Racers

The GTA in its hey-day. Han Akersloot's 1300 GTA Junior vies with a Capri for track position at Silverstone, June 1970. (Courtesy Ian Catt)

The Giulia GT was such a competitive racing car in its heyday that it was only natural that it would have a new lease of life in the classic racing arena. The most high-profile international series is the FIA Cup for Historic Touring Cars, which has been running for many years. In 2002 it included rounds at Anderstorp, Zolder, Dijon, the Nürburgring, Mondello Park and Imola. All the races are run as one-hour events with a change of drivers, each having to be at the wheel for at least 20 minutes to qualify. To an extent this series replicates the European Touring Car races of the 1960s, which were generally 500km affairs. In the UK, 105-Series cars have featured in HSCC events, but the AutoItalia and AROC series, from 2002 operating as the Alfa Romeo Championship Association,

Tony Dron drove one of the Penthouse 1600 GT Juniors at Brands Hatch during the 1975 Race of Champions meeting.
(Courtesy Ian Catt)

generally field grids of more modern cars. In 2001, there was only one Giulia coupé in the AROC/ARCA series, the Gregor Truscott 2000 GTV that passed on to James Diffey.

More relevantly, one of the most challenging post-historic championships to emerge in recent years is the Top Hat challenge, which has also managed to recreate much of the flavour of saloon car racing in the mid- to late-1960s. Launched in 1998 by classic car specialist and Alfa-buff Julius Thurgood, the popular Top Hat Group 2 historic touring car series invariably featured a fairly broad spectrum of Alfas, and Giulia GTs in particular.

You can leave your hat on

The Top Hat historic race series is unique in that it fields as many as 250 competitors competing in five separate races during one meeting. With over 1400 racing members registered, Top Hat is one of the most strongly supported series in European historic racing. By 2002, the Top Hat challenge also included an endurance series catering for older historic touring cars like those that contested the British Saloon Car Championship in the 1950s, such as Jack Sears' Austin Westminster 105, Jeff Uren's Ford Zephyr Mk. II, Les Leston's Riley 1.5 and 'Doc' Shepherd's Austin A40. Other entries included the works-prepared Jaguar Mk. VIIs and Speedwell-tuned Austin A35s, conducted with indecent haste by Graham Hill. To achieve a parity of sorts and to help recreate the handling of the period, all cars were

The Belgian VDS team's GTAs in the paddock at the Snetterton round of the European Touring Car Championship in 1966, with pole-man John Whitmore (right) on foot. (Courtesy Ian Catt)

They're at it again! The GTA identity was revived for the Super Touring Alfa 156 in 2002. Here, the works' Nordauto squad of reigning champion Fabrizio Giovanardi and Nicola Larini dominate the ETCC round at Magny Cours in April 2002, when the Schnitzer BMW 320is and Prodrive Volvo S60s could do nothing about them. For 2003, the Autodelta name was revived for the works' Nordauto race team. (Courtesy Alfa Romeo)

Giulia TI Super leads a Giulia Coupé and an Imp in a Top Hat round.

Conceived as a lightweight road-racer, the TZ1 - Tubolare Zagato - used the 1600 unit from the TI Super saloon with 45 DCOE Weber carbs and special sump and gearbox bellhousing.

Robert Petersson in his 2.0-litre GT Am replica stays ahead of a BDA-powered Mk II Lotus Cortina at Mantorp Park in 1997. (Courtesy Gunar Johansson)

Norwich-based Alfa specialist Richard Drake fits original 9 x 13in Tipo 33 magnesium wheels to a Jonathan Smith-built GT Am replica. The task required specially-made longer studs and spacers to accommodate the offset of the big wheels, plus shortened steering arms, similar to those marketed by Autodelta in the 1960s, courtesy of EB Spares. (Author's photo)

This 1750 GTV was transformed into a GT Am-style track-day and race car by Jonathan Smith at Cawston, Norfolk. (Author's photo)

This 2000 GTV shell has its bulging GT Am plastic arches fitted prior to painting and fettling as a race car. The moulds were taken from the wing extensions of a GTA 1300 Junior. (Courtesy Robert Petersson)

to use Dunlop CR65 'L' or 'M' section historic racing tyres.

The 2002 Top Hat series got under way with the H&H Historic Race Festival at Donington in May, crossing the channel in early July to top the bill at the newly revived Chimay circuit on the Franco-Belgian border. At the beginning of September came the Donington Italian Race Festival, followed by a classic 1-hour endurance race on the fast Spa-Francorchamps circuit in Belgium. The finale was staged at the H&H Historic Race Weekend at Snetterton in October.

For 2002, however, Julius Thurgood's brain child was the GTA Challenge. This was a race exclusively for GTAs and GTA-lookalikes. The five-race series was open to any owner of an Alfa Romeo 105-series coupé, from a base-model 1300GT to a full-blooded GT Am. Julius explained: 'I'm keen that everyone who wants to take part can access the series, and therefore an open-door policy will be applied. That'll make the owner of a hybrid GTA replica

The 1966 Sprint GT Veloce of Dr Bernardo Martinez competes against a variety of classic machinery in the Watkins Glen Enduro 2001 event. At the Mid-Ohio Vintage Meeting, June 15/16, 2002, it won the Enduro and placed second in the Sprint race.

Based on the externally identical Giulietta Sprint Speciale, the pretty Giulia SS was available in small numbers between 1963 and 1966 with the Veloce-spec 1600cc motor.

This 1972 2000 Berlina sports flared wheelarches and has its headlight apertures plated over. Formerly a Bobcor race car, it belongs to Dr Bernardo Martinez and is competing at Watkins Glen during the Enduro 2001 meeting.

This 1969 GTA is the ex-Bobcor TransAm car, pictured in a classic race at Mid Ohio in 2002. This car ran in the US TransAm series in 1971 and 1972, driven by Ken Schley, who trailered the car from race to race behind a converted coach. Running as number 8 in 1971, it was painted red, and Schley placed fifth in the championship. He was recruited by the Bobcor team from Buffalo, New York in 1972 and, accordingly, the car was painted yellow, racing under the number 52. Former US rally star John Buffum drove it in one race in 1972. In 1974 it was painted white and its wheelarches were extended and it was entered as a 1300 GTA by Walter Vandenberg in SCCA events in '74 and '75. From 1976 to 1978 it was driven in SCCA races by Andy Scopazzi from San Francisco, and in total the car knotched up 29 wins in SCCA events between 1974 and 1978.

The 116-series Alfetta GTV succeeded the 105-series Giulia coupés.

Winter testing at Goodwood prior to the five-round international Thorogood GTA Challenge. In 2003, competitors could race at Donington Park (Ferrari Festival), Zandvoort (Alfa Romeo Festival), Chimay (Belgian Historic Festival), Spa (Six Hours), and Mallory Park (Top Hat Race Day).

In 2003, owners of Giulia Sprint GTs and GTAs could enter the Thorogood GTA Challenge. There were three categories: Strada for low-budget, road-going cars; Corsa for race-prepared pre-'65 FIA Appendix K Group 2 specification cars; and Romeo for 750- and 101-series Giulietta and Giulia models.

In 2002, the Top Hat series brought together a fantastic array of racing saloons from the 1960s, ranging from agile Giulia Sprint GTs and Lotus Cortinas to Mk II Jaguar and plenty of buzz-boxes.

just as welcome as a collector who wants to field his original ex-Works Autodelta GT Am race car. So, track-prepared road cars will be as welcome as purpose-built race-cars. I shall make every effort to promote the true spirit of the period, and owners are encouraged to emulate the liveries that defined the cars in their original period.'

In order to create more of a level playing field, classes were divided into the engine capacity sizes of the production series, 1300, 1600, 1750 and 2000, and competitors were free to use any RAC MSA recognised road-treaded tyre, but not slicks. To get the series off the ground it was clear that anything wearing a Bertone coupé body would get a race, and it looked likely that specifications would be tightened up for 2003.

There are at least half-a-dozen regular Giulia GTs of one sort or another competing regularly in the Top Hat series - from Sprint GTs to GTAs and GT Am replicas. Any Bertone coupé can enter the GTA Challenge, and Julius was talking about a class for the Giulia Super and TI saloons, for which both he and I have a soft spot. The GTA Challenge certainly has huge appeal, in the same way that the Dutch Squadra Bianca fleet of Giulia saloons does - an entire 32 car field of Supers hurtling into Tarzan hairpin at Zandvoort is an awesome sight indeed. In Julius Thurgood's GTA Challenge entries for genuine GTAs and their ilk included cars from Jon Shipman, Nick Savage, Richard Frankl, Peter Sugden, Richard Banks, Andrew Thorogood, the ex-Spider's Web GTA, Jim Evans, Ivor

Miller, Steven Chase's wide-bodied car, and Tim Dutton's ex-Autodelta car as driven in 1966 by Jochen Rindt. The first round of the GTA Challenge at Donington Park was won by Andrew Banks in a 2.0-litre TwinSpark-powered car, which was very much in the spirit of the Alfa Romeo engine-swapping tradition, even if it wasn't an authentic GTA.

Over in Sweden, where they take FIA Appendix K more seriously than most, a typical example of a successful classic racing project with a Giulia Sprint GT was that of Swedish motoring journalist Robert Petersson, whose day job is deputy editor of the excellent *Auto Motor & Sport* monthly. In a nutshell, he turned a 1973 2000 GTV into a 1750 GT Am lookalike, and set about trouncing the Scandinavian classic touring cars. And, as if that's not enough, Robert has also owned an ex-works GTA, and currently races a 1600 Sprint GT.

Swedish race prep

The following account of the race preparation of Robert's GT Am provides a glimpse into the build process of a classic Alfa Romeo racing car, albeit at a strictly amateur level - no disrespect in that, as it demonstrates what can be done on a fairly modest budget. This car was built to a set of rules peculiar to Sweden. Although normally adhering strictly to appendix K regulations, in this case the national classic 1966-1972 series used an amalgam of appendix K and Swedish Group 2 rules from the period. That meant that the car held national FIA papers as a Group 2 1971 2000 GTV. This was because for the

national regulations, the identity or year of manufacture meant nothing so long as the car complied with the homologation form. It followed, then, that Robert Petersson's team could not use GT Am papers as it didn't use the narrow-angle cylinder head. On the other hand, Petersson's team was obliged to adhere to the 2000 GTV's minimum weight of 975 kilos. The Swedish Historic 1966-72 Championship runs classes for up to 1300cc, 1300-1600cc, 1600-2000cc, and over 2000cc classes, and full points are awarded in each class if there are over five starters (otherwise half points are awarded).

When Robert bought the car it was already being used for track days, had a roll-cage installed and a mildly-tuned engine. He only had to add the wing extensions and replace the front grille with a 1750 GTV item, therefore, to make it look like a GT Am.

The race prep was carried out by Bo Johansson in his workshop - formerly a Baptist Chapel - at Hällestad, near Finspång. He also restored one of the Team Topcon GTA 1300 Juniors that were seen in the UK at Silverstone in the TT in 1971-1972. In 1999 the restored Topcon car was due to be sold to Japan, and Robert Petersson was testing it at Mantorp Park circuit prior to delivery. The occasion was a Swedish Alfa Club meeting, and everyone cheered as he blasted along the pit straight using 9000rpm in third and fourth. In the excitement he forgot all about restrictions and, as he reached the main straight and hit 9000rpm in fifth, the bonnet came adrift and blew

The cockpit of Robert Petersson's GT Am replica is still recognisably a 2000 GTV, with the race seat, alloy foot-rest, fire extinguisher and ignition cut-off testifying to its real purpose. (Courtesy Robert Petersson)

Bo Johnsson inspects the engine bay of his GTA 1600 during fettling and race preparation at Bo Johansson's workshop. (Courtesy Robert Petersson)

From left to right, Robert Petersson's 1600 Sprint GT, Bo Johansson's GTA 1300 Junior, and Petersson's GT Am replica. The workshop is Johansson's, formerly a Baptist Church. He previously restored two other GTA 1300 Juniors, including Ragnar Segring's Team Topcon car that ran at Silverstone in 1971-72. (Courtesy Robert Petersson)

This 2.0-litre twin-cam is destined for Robert Petersson's GT Am lookalike. Note the 48 Weber carbs and extra ventilation at the front to stop oil leaks. (Courtesy Robert Petersson)

away. It took 20 minutes to find it in the woods, but it was so bent that Johansson had to make a new skin for it. The old one decorates the wall of his workshop. At the time of this track test, the Topcon car was still owned by one of its original drivers, Ragnar Segring, who was later team manager for the Topcon team. Ragnar worked for the company that owned the track, which made flouting the noise regulations possible. Fitted with an open exhaust, the engine really screamed over 9000rpm.

This is the rebuilt GTA 1300 Junior engine from Bo Johansson's car, awaiting reinstatement. (Courtesy Robert Petersson)

Bo Johansson's garage contains his own GTA 1300 Junior, since sold to Portugal. It ran in Holland for most of its active life and was imported to Sweden and crashed in the late 1980s. During its rebuild, Bo consulted Carlo Chiti who even remembered the set-up pressures for the injection pump. Car 38 is Robert Petersson's GT Am. (Courtesy Robert Petersson)

The front suspension assembly of the GT Am replica, showing the Tar-Ox solid discs and callipers with Pagid pads, adjustable top-links and Koni dampers. (Courtesy Robert Petersson)

A set of 16-hole GTA alloy wheels shod with Goodyear period racing tyres ready for fitting on Bo Johnsson's 1600 GTA. The Sprint GT (65) is also running GTA wheels. (Courtesy Robert Petersson)

Underside of Robert Petersson's GT Am replica, showing the Panhard-rod fitted to locate the axle sideways. He found that the GTA-type sliding block-location didn't work very well unless the suspension was made so stiff that it became hard to get the power down on bumpy Swedish racetracks. (Courtesy Robert Petersson)

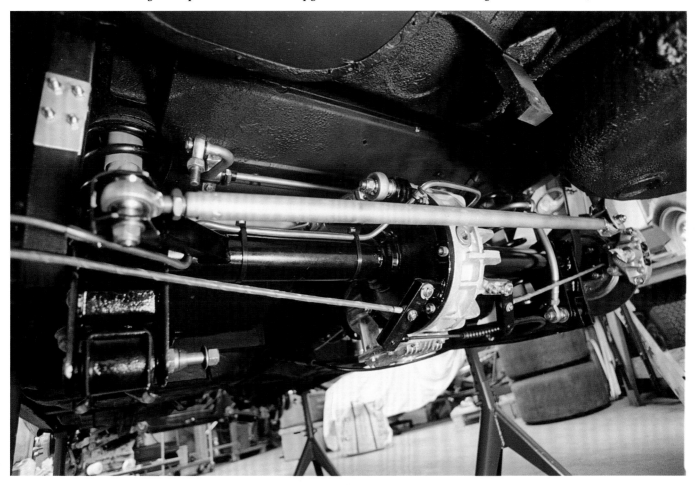

The 2.0-litre engine in Petersson's GT Am replica was built by Alfa Romeo and race-engine specialists GreySteel in Stockholm. It breathed though twin Weber 48s, and was equipped with custom-made camshafts and exhaust manifolds. Otherwise, it was normally ported and very carefully balanced. It developed between 195-200bhp and revved to 7300-7400rpm.

According to Robert Petersson, 'The important thing was torque, though. Everything that was done to it was with torque as first priority. One of the reasons was that we used a standard ratio gearbox. The rear axle ratio was at first 5.125:1 but that was totally wrong – I spent a lot of time in fifth and the gearbox was not up to it. The small fifth gear axle could not

take the torque. After that we went to a 4.3:1 Berlina ratio, but even that was a bit off; it probably would have been right with a close ratio box, but as it was the car was quickest with a standard GTV 4.1:1 axle. Of course, we also tightened the limited-slip diff, but without locking it completely.'

The most significant improvement came when the chassis was sorted,

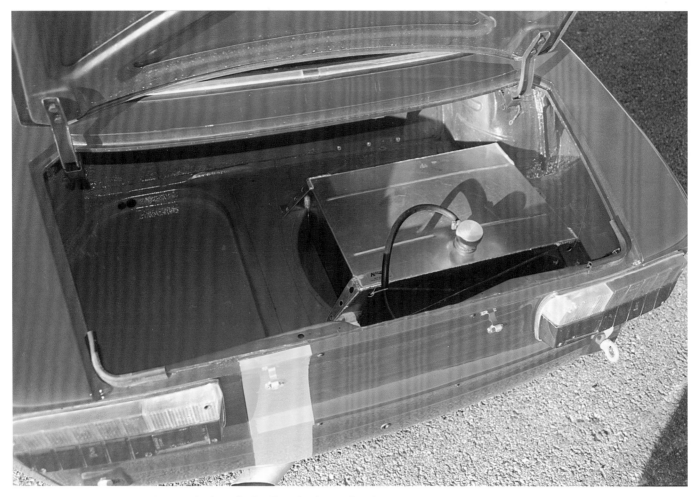

Racing 36-litre fuel cell in the boot of Robert Petersson's GT Am replica.

however. 9 x 13in Tipo 33 magnesium wheels, which were also used on GT Ams, were fitted. They had eight wheels that were crack-tested before use, and shod with Dunlop Clubman slicks running higher pressures than the lightweight Clubmans cars. For wet races they used Compomotive 8 x 13in Minilite-lookalikes, which apparently suited the car admirably, being both quick and long-lasting. Bolting them on wasn't quite that straightforward, though. As Robert explained, 'One problem we had was that the 2000 GTV's brakes didn't fit inside the small 13-inch wheels. We had to go for smaller ones – GT Am aluminium callipers would have been

Robert Petersson's 2.0-litre GT Am replica leads a 2.6-litre Köln Capri lookalike at Mantorp Park in 1998. (Courtesy Gunar Johansson)

144

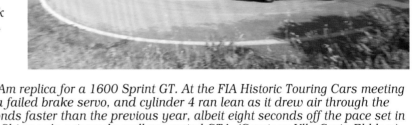

High in the Sicilian countryside, a GT Am rounds Ganza hairpins during the Targa Florio centenary meeting, 2006. (Courtesy Antony Fraser)

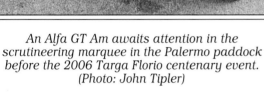

An Alfa GT Am awaits attention in the scrutineering marquee in the Palermo paddock before the 2006 Targa Florio centenary event. (Photo: John Tipler)

For 2001, Robert Petersson exchanged his GT Am replica for a 1600 Sprint GT. At the FIA Historic Touring Cars meeting at Anderstorp in 2002, he was troubled by a failed brake servo, and cylinder 4 ran lean as it drew air through the vacuum tube. He still managed to run two seconds faster than the previous year, albeit eight seconds off the pace set in the European Cup race by Mark Hales in Jon Shipman's extremely well-presented GTA. (Courtesy Ulla-Carin Ekblom)

The GTA of John Shipman and Mark Hales in its paddock enclave at Spa-Francorchamps during to the Six Hours meeting.
(Photo: John Tipler)

A classic shot of a GT Am roaring through the streets of Collesano during the 2006 Targa Florio centenary event.
(Courtesy Antony Fraser)

The French 2000 GTV of Thierry Guichaoua and Marc Hardy came 18th in general classification on the 2006 Carrera Panamericana.
(Courtesy Kenneth Olausson)

The Guichaoua/Hardy 2000 GTV at speed on the Huatasco stage near Tehuacán during the seven-day, 2,000-mile trans-Mexican Carrera Panamericana.
(Photo: John Tipler)

GTA Junior speeding through the Sicilian countryside between Scillato and Collesano on a 72km lap of the Targa Florio circuit, 2006.
(Courtesy Antony Fraser)

ideal. We tried normal 1600 brakes – in fact, we used the whole 1600 assembly including hub-carriers, steering-arms, and with these standard callipers we used Tar-Ox solid 1600 discs and Pagid pads. With the help of a Tilton brake balance adjuster the brake performance was stunning, which shows that size is not everything!'

Using the 1600 GT's front uprights had one more advantage. The separate, bolted steering arms made it much easier to adjust bump-steer. They simply replaced them with a bendable bar and adjusted geometry on the garage-floor until they were satisfied with it, and then replaced the originals with new items bent at the same angle. Otherwise, the front suspension had adjustable top-links and GTA-extensions that increased negative camper on bump. The rear-axle was more of a problem. Said Robert, 'It wasn't until we replaced the upper Y-link with a GTA-like simple arm and mounted a Panhard-rod to locate the axle sideways that we hit gold. The standard, or even the GTA-type sliding block-location, does not work very well unless you stiffen the suspension to the point where it's hard to get the power down, at least not on our bumpy Swedish tracks. The Panhard-rod is allowed in our national 1966-72 Group regs, and that solved all that. For shock absorbers we used Konis that were specially-valved for the car.'

The GT Am was probably at its best during the 1999 season, by which time they'd sorted out the gearing. The highlight of its career was at the very complex Gelleråsen circuit at Karlskoga, which also has an extremely long straight, in June 1999. The practice was wet-dry-wet-dry, but Robert managed to claim outright pole position in both conditions, beating a bunch of full-house 3.0-litre Capris, a handful of BDA-engined 1800 Escorts and a Lotus Cortina. The pole-time was 1m 18sec in dry practice, at a time when the quickest works Volvos and Nissans in Super Touring were doing 1m 06sec. The race was wet, and after some 25 minutes racing Robert was overall winner by some 20 seconds. That was the car's only outright win, but a lot of 2.0-litre class wins secured overall victory in the series, both in 1998 and 1999. 'For 2000 we went a bit too far trying for more power,' said Robert, 'and after I put the car in the barriers at Knutstorp in July it was never the same again.'

The GT Am was subsequently sold to an owner in Denmark and, at the time of writing, Robert and Bo Johansson were dreaming up a new GT Am project. Meanwhile, Robert campaigned a totally restored 1600 Sprint GT with rebuilt engine and Gozzoli-sourced close-ratio gears in Swedish national events. The impending GT Am project would mean that the Sprint GT would have to go to a new home and, as I write this, I'm seriously considering taking it on.

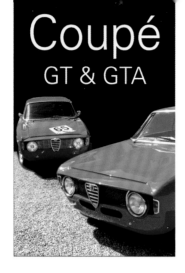

Gunze Sangyo's GTAm.

Appendix 1

Alfa Romeo Models

I know hardly a single Alfa Romeo fan who doesn't have at least a small collection of scale models of his favourite Alfas. From after-school hours with Airfix kits, I've certainly never been able to kick the habit and today, after a number of changes of address, lifestyle and so on, I have perhaps a couple of dozen models, which are mostly Alfas and largely 1/43rd scale. There are plenty of people who would regard this as a very modest show indeed. Model collecting is best rationalised according to your ability as a model builder, available space and, perhaps most crucial, disposable budget. The 'ready-made' die-cast metal models are the best bet if you have neither the time nor the skill to do justice to the resin or white metal kits by companies like Provence Moulage, Tron, BBR or Alezan.

Resin and white metal kits are not particularly hard to assemble because, at around 1/43rd scale, they are too small for the inclusion of sophisticated mechanical details. However, they do offer superb reproduction of the original car's shape and external detail, so finish is all and a first rate paint job

is essential. You'll need to be geared up with scalpel and spray-can and to have the patience to apply several very thin coats of paint. I think the most frustrating thing about resin and white metal kits is that there is often a certain amount of pruning of the resin to be done in order to get certain bits together; for instance, when I was building a 6C 3000 CM, getting the interior to fit inside the bodyshell took some fairly savage hacking. These models are relatively expensive but, if representing a racing car, usually come with sophisticated decals to mimic a specific race. For instance, you could get a model of Toine Hezemans' GTAm exactly as it appeared in the 1970 TT at Silverstone.

Die-cast mass production models are a lot less versatile in respect of customised racing cars but are much cheaper. Die-casts in 1/43rd scale are often really inexpensive but accurate enough to represent very good value. 1/24th scale cars are also excellent value, offering a lot of car for your money, but do take up a lot of space. It's often a good discipline to rationalise your collection to a particular model, marque or theme of car. A friend of mine, model producer and collector Paul Nieuwenhius, specialises in coach-builders and has a comprehensive collection of Zagato-bodied cars, from Lancia to Aston Martin. If your models are going to look good en-masse, it's

best to stick to one size, and I find the old Dinky/Corgi 1/43rd scale is quite convenient.

Another way of collecting the very best 1/43rd models, especially if you haven't the time or the inclination to put them together, is to go direct to a specialist model shop and buy one of their display items, or get an expert to build one for you. In Alfa Romeo Owners' Club circles, Ed McDonough is probably your man, and he will also supply Alfa models to order, either in kit form or ready made. The latter is obviously going to be significantly dearer, but you do get a first class job. For anyone interested, Ed runs Alfa Models from 9 Green Lane, Wootton, Northants, NG4 0HG.

Other Alfa Romeo model specialists are Milestone Miniatures, MPH Models and Model Masters of The Old Dairy Studio, Trevor Mill Cottage, Llangollen, Clwyd, Wales. In Germany contact Jürgen Prüfect, Alfa Modell Club, Eichenhof 4, 4100 Duisburg 1, Germany.

I have also dealt with Grand Prix Models, of 167 Watling Street, Radlett, Herts, Telephone 0923 852828, and their service is always prompt; they publish a newsletter called *Four Small Wheels*, which is right up to date with colour pictures of the latest models. *Model Auto Revue* is similarly on the ball.

Ed McDonough very kindly provided the following 'fairly thorough' list of Alfa coupé models relevant to this book,

Top,Verem's TZ, centre, Provence Moulage's GTA and below, the same company's TZ2.

each complete with scale and, where known, model number.

1954 2000 Sportiva
1/43, Replicars 101

1962 2600 Sprint Coupé
1/43, Politoys 537 & 514
1/43, T billssi (USSR) 7
1/43, Dalia 23125
1/43, Solido 125

1963 Giulia Sprint Speciale
1/66, Penny Policars 026
1/43, Politoys 506
1/43, Kiev 6 (3 variations)
1/43, Idal 112
1/43, Joal 112
1/23, Togi

1963 Giulia Sprint GT
1/43, Editoys 1
1/43, Mercury 40
1/43, Mercury 40b
1/66, Penny 28
1/66, Penny 46
1/20, Pocher (plastic)
1/43, Politoys 500
1/23, Togi
1/23, Togi (kit)

1/43, Merkloos (plastic)
1/50, Merkloos (plastic)
1/43, Progetto 041 (4 colour variations)

1964 Giulia Sprint 1300 GT
1/43, Progetto

1964 Giulia TZ
1/43, Verem 148

1964 Canguro
1/24, F & N (plastic)
1/43, Joal 105
1/40, Kawai 4 (plastic)
1/43, Mercury 29 & 29b
1/24, Midori (plastic)
1/66, Penny 22
1/43, Politoys 526
1/43, Politoys 527
1/43, Politoys 529
1/43, Politoys 539
1/25, Hasegawa (plastic kit)
1/40, Kawai Atlas (plastic kit)

1965 Giulia Sprint GTA
1/43, Bracco 1 (resin)
1/43, FDS 13 (1300 Junior)
1/43, Progetto 9 (1300 Junior)
1/43, Provence Moulage 46 (resin kit)
1/23, Togi 110
1/23, Togi 228 (kit)
1/23 Gunze Sangyo
1/43, Progetto 042 (Corsa)
1/43, Century 7
1/43, Barnini 02

1966 Giulia Sprint GTV 1600
1/23, Togi 112
1/23, Togi 230 (kit)
1/43, Century
1/43, Politoys 500

1966 Giulia GT 1300 Junior
1/55, Polistil RJ45
1/41, Politoys 80 (plastic)
1/23, Togi 111
1/23, Togi 229 (kit)
1/72, GCCG (plastic)
1/48, Grisoni (plastic)
1/41, McGregor N80 (plastic)

1971 Junior Zagato
1/43, Verem 183

1971 2000 GTV
1/43, Spec Box 849

1965-67 TZ2
1/43 Provence Moulage (resin kit)

1970 Montreal
1/43, DRS
1/43, Eco Design 1012 (resin)
1/43, Outercars 307
1/43, Mercury 304
1/43, Nacoral 307
1/43, Norev 179 (plastic)
1/43, Norev 816
1/24, Otaki (plastic)
1/22, Pocher (plastic)
1/25, Politoys S-6
1/16, Re-E1 (plastic)
1/60, Siku V-321
1/60, Siku 1025
1/23, Togi 116
1/23, Togi 234
1/43, Dates (resin)
1/43, Dris
1/25, Polistil 524

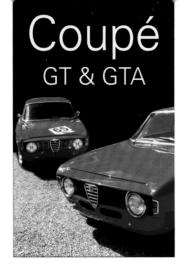

Coupé
GT & GTA

Appendix 2

Alfa Romeo
Giulia Coupé
Official Production
Figures

MODEL	YEARS	UNITS BUILT
Giulia 1600 Sprint	1962-1964	7107
Giulia Sprint Speciale	1963-1965	1400
Giulia Sprint GT	1963-1966	21542
Giulia Sprint 1300	1964-1966	1900
Giulia Sprint GTA	1965-1969	500
Giulia Sprint GT Veloce	1966-1968	14240
Giulia GT 1300 Junior	1966-1972	80623
Giulia Sprint GTA SA	1967-1968	10
1750 GT Veloce	1967-1972	41780
1750 GT Veloce America	1968-1972	2475
GTA 1300 Junior	1968-1972	447
GTAm	1970-1971	40
2000 GTV	1970-1977	37459

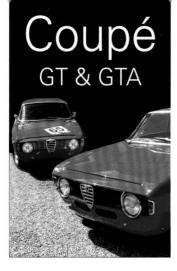

Coupé
GT & GTA

Appendix 3

Alfa Romeo Giulia Coupé Advertisments

Not the kind of ad you'd see today. Dating from 1970, the ad celebrates Christine Beckers' 3rd place in the Nürburgring 6-Hours of July 11th. Great emphasis is placed on the similarities between the 1750GT Veloce and 2-litre GTAm.

A girl hasn't done it before.
Christine Beckers
did it in an Alfa Romeo.

Two remarkable events happened in the 6-hour saloon car race at Nurburgring on July 11. Alfa Romeo notched up an impressive 1-2-3 win. And the third Alfa was driven by a girl. Which says a lot about her driving—and about her car.

All three winning cars were Alfa Romeo 2-litre GTams which are having such a success this season. The engine is a stretched version of the 1750 twin-cam engine fitted as standard in the Alfa Romeo 1750 GT Veloce.

Andrea de Adamich and his partner Gianluigi Picchi completed 38 laps (538.9 miles) to take 1st. And knocked an astounding 12.1 secs off the touring car lap record (previously held by Dieter Quester in a BMW).

Dieter Mohr and Hans Hessel filled 2nd place.

And Christine Beckers, partnered by Teodoro Zeccoli, showed the rest her tail-lights to take 3rd. A girl hasn't done it before.

This 1-2-3 for Alfa at the 'Ring follows the success of similar Alfa GTams in taking three out of the first six places at Silverstone in June. It keeps Alfa firmly in the lead in the European Touring Car Challenge with both 1st (GTam 2-litre) and 2nd (GT 1300) places, a BMW 2800 following behind in third. (Subject to official confirmation.)

Alfa's leading position results from racing experience dating back nearly 50 years. Through continuous development under the most gruelling racing conditions, exceptional qualities of stamina, performance and safety are built into every Alfa.

You might not want to race your own Alfa. But it's good to know it's bred to win.

ALFA ROMEO NETWORK OF DEALERS

BEDFORDSHIRE
F H Moss (Garages) Ltd
Tel. No: Luton (0582) 28521 2 3
BERKSHIRE
The Forge Motor Co
Tel. No: Bourne End (06285) 22984
BUCKINGHAMSHIRE
Milbourne Garage Ltd
Tel. No: Challont St. Giles (0240 7) 2351
Russel Motor Services. Tel. No: Naphill (024024) 3270
CAMBRIDGESHIRE
Maloney & Rhodes Ltd.
Tel. No: Cambridge (0223) 47268
CHESHIRE
The Northern Performance Car Centre.
Tel. No: Lower Peover (0565 81) 2899
Mainolotts Holdings Ltd.
Tel. No: Chester (0244) 42277 8
CORNWALL
Cotswold Garage. Tel. No: Fowey (072s 83) p4h8
DERBYSHIRE
Deryck K. Morley Ltd. Tel. No: Ilkeston (06072) 3513
Ovar Motors. Tel. No: Derby (0332) 32421 22
DEVON
Seymour Horwell Garage Ltd.
Tel. No: Newton Abbot (0626) 2545
DORSET
Rob Walker Hushams Garage Ltd.
Tel. No: Parkstone 6145
CO. DURHAM
Mill Garages Ltd
Tel. No: Sunderland (0783) 57631
ESSEX
Grange Motors Ltd. Tel. No: Brentwnud 216161
GLOUCESTERSHIRE
Cotham Hill Garage Ltd. Tel. No: Bristol (0272) 24401
Mynd House Motors Ltd.
Tel. No: Gloucester (0452) 25251 3
HAMPSHIRE
Quadrioglio Motors Ltd.
Tel. No: Southampton (0703) 29003
R. F. Seward Ltd. Tel. No: Southampton (0703) 72431-5
HERTFORDSHIRE
Richard Redgrave Ltd.
Tel. No: Hemel Hempstead (0442) 51466
KENT
Sundridge Park Motors Ltd. Tel. No: 01-857 2293 4
Berners Hill Garage Ltd.
Tel. No: Yeomans Grange 2772
LANCASHIRE
Kings Hall Motor Co. Ltd
Tel. No: Blackpool (0253) 25654
Molyneux West & Co. Ltd.
Tel. No: Manchester (061) 748 5919 2771
Westwood Garage Ltd.
Tel. No: Great Harwood (0254 87) 2202 2744
Charlie Oates Ltd. Tel. No: Carnforth (052 473) 2460
LEICESTERSHIRE
Grebe Garage Ltd. Tel. No: Leicester (0533) 29345
Lazenby Garage Ltd. Tel. No: Rothley (0533 24) 2484
LINCOLNSHIRE
F. K. Sharpe Ltd. Tel. No: Lincoln (0522) 22329
LONDON
Belgravia Service Garage. Tel. No: 01-235 6344
Bradshaw Webb & Co. Tel. No: 01-493 7705
Chipstead of Kensington Ltd. Tel. No: 01-727 0611
Alan Day Ltd. Tel. No: 01-435 1133
Hexagon of Highgate Ltd. Tel. No: 01-340 3431
The Italian Car Centre. Tel. No: 01-709 8860
Motorture Ltd. Tel. No: 01-569 1166 0081
M T C (Cars) Ltd. Tel. No: 01-727 3445
Portman Garages Ltd. Tel. No: 01-935 5415
MIDDLESEX
Toombs Ltd Tel. No: Staines (01-79) 51927

NORFOLK
A. J. S (Car Sales) Ltd. Tel. No: Norwich (0603) 43643
Kitchen Bros. Tel. No: Diss (0379) 3141
NORTHAMPTONSHIRE
Dove of Northampton Ltd
Tel. No: Northampton (0604) 38411
Peter Bugg Motors Ltd. Tel. No: Glinton (0731 6) 351
NORTHUMBERLAND
Hilton Brothers Ltd.
Tel. No: Newcastle-upon-Tyne (0632) 869118
NOTTINGHAMSHIRE
Sytner of Mapperley
Tel. No: Nottingham (0602) 63321 2
OXFORDSHIRE
Motorword Garages Ltd
Tel. No: Kidlington (00965) 3732
SOMERSET
Benter Motors Ltd. Tel. No: Bath (0225) 23050
STAFFORDSHIRE
E. L. Bouts Motors Ltd.
Tel. No: Wolverhampton (0902) 23295
Archway Garage Ltd.
Tel. No: Stoke-on-Trent (0782) 32566 33618
SURREY
Thomson & Taylor (Brooklands) Ltd.
Tel. No: Cobham (0-266) 4493
Normand Ltd. Tel. No: Horley (02934) 2257
Rardley (Continental) Ltd. Tel. No: Hindhead 1233
SUSSEX
Seven Dials Motors Grand Service Station Ltd.
Tel. No: Brighton (0273) 684921
Berners Hill Garage Ltd. Tel. No: Flimwell 256
Greenwood Garage Ltd. Tel. No: Slindon (0243 65) 289
WARWICKSHIRE
Hawthorne Garage Ltd.
Tel. No: Birmingham (021) 353 1345
Mario Deirotti Ltd.
Tel. No: Birmingham (021) 772 0759
Ulverley Garage.
Tel. No: Birmingham (021) 706 4095 1165
WILTSHIRE
Rob Walker Corsley Garage Ltd.
Tel. No: Chapmanslade (0373 88) 383
Bath Road Garage. Tel. No: Swindon (0793) 3586
YORKSHIRE
Moortown Motors Ltd.
Tel. No: Leeds (0532) 31894
Alwyn Kershaw. Tel. No: York (0904) 22772
The Trinity Garage Co. Ltd
Tel. No: Huddersfield (0484) 20822
NORTH WALES
L. S. P. Motors Ltd. Tel. No: Llandudno (0492) 81001
SOUTH WALES
Andrews Garage. Tel. No: Cardiff (0222) 24422
SCOTLAND
Hamilton Bros. Ltd
Tel. No: Halfway (041 882) 3221
John Rutherford & Sons Ltd.
Tel. No: Earlston (089 684) 326
Doontoot Garages Ltd. Tel. No: Alloway (02921) 42342
Fishers Garage Ltd. Tel. No: Edinburgh (031) 229 5561
Frank Callander Motors Ltd.
Tel. No: Glasgow (041) 946 5124
George Strathdee Jnr. Tel. No: Aberdeen (0224) 30181
NORTHERN IRELAND
Malcolm Templeton. Tel. No: Ballymena (0266) 2161 2
Malcolm Templeton. Tel. No: Belfast (0232) 27269
CHANNEL ISLANDS
Henry Linton Cars Ltd.
Tel. No: Jersey Central (0534) 33511
EIRE
McCairns Motors Ltd. Tel. No: Dublin 379933

Alfa Romeo (G.B.) Ltd, Edgware Road (Nr. Staples Corner), London NW2 01-450 8641

Would the gentleman who spent 10 mins. staring at the Alfa 1750 GTV please read this ad.

This one is for you if you normally look at the Alfa 1750 GTV through a showroom window.

We often see you standing there.

Just as often we see you park your car outside. And, just out of habit, we place a rough valuation on it. And we think, yes, that's a very good start to owning an Alfa.

But you just stand there. You don't come in.

So here are the answers to a few of the questions that must have occured to you on the other side of the glass.

Price: Experience tells us that you over-estimated it. You probably put it at about £3,500. Well, the correct price is £2,248 tax paid. The 1750 is the most expensive Alfa. The 1300 GT costs a bit less and still manages an easy 103 mph. It costs £1,748.

Trade-in valuations: Here you probably under-estimated the worth of your present car. It could

cost you a good deal less to make the change than you think.

Technical: This you probably know. But just to sum it up: The Alfa 1750 GTV has an aluminium engine, twin overhead cams, and disc brakes all round. Top speed is 118 mph at 5,500 rpm. But we've got a free booklet that tells the story better.

Servicing: Your precious Alfa will only be serviced by men who have passed the rigorous Alfa Romeo training course. You'll find them at over 100 Alfa dealers throughout the country.

Export: If you're an overseas visitor, find out about our own personal export scheme. We've got attractive facilities for tax and duty-free purchases.

Test Drives: We actually like people to take our cars for a test drive. In certain circumstances, you can even borrow one for 24 hours, just to get the feel of it. Your Alfa dealer would be very happy for you to take an Alfa, any Alfa, for a test drive. Write to, or phone Alfa Romeo, 164 Sloane Street, London, S.W.1. 01-235 7746. Reverse the charges if you like.

Alfa Romeo

Introducing the latest Alfa Romeo. The 2000 GT Veloce.

The new Alfa Romeo 2000 GT Veloce is a sports car. Hence its impeccable performance, which you'll discover when you drive it.

The 1962cc twin overhead camshaft alloy engine has twin carburettors, develops 150 bhp, and effortlessly powers you to 121 mph. On the way, you'll use today's most precise five speed gearbox.

And discover Alfa Romeo's famous roadholding. Provided by a live rear axle, anti-roll bars front and rear, and HR high speed radials.

To stop you, there's a four disc, dual circuit servo assisted braking system.

Inside, you'll notice other things. Like the reclining, anatomically designed bucket seats, lavish dashboard and centre console. Two speed heating and ventilation. Two speed windscreen wipers. Cigar lighter.

If you wish, your own 2000 GTV can also be equipped with a heated rear screen, electric tinted windows and air conditioning. A limited slip differential, to further the effect of cornering on rails.

Visit your dealer, and see the new 2000 range. You'll like what you drive.

2000 GT Veloce (Pictured).
2+2. From £2439.
2000 Saloon.
Seats 4/5. From £2026.
2000 Spider Veloce.
Seats 2. From £2439.

Alfa Romeo Alfa Romeo (GB) Ltd., Edgware Road (nr. Staples Corner), London NW2 6LX. 01-450 8641.

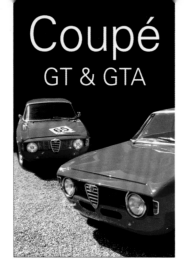

Coupé
GT & GTA

Appendix 4
Specialist Directory

Owners and prospective buyers of Alfa Romeo Giulia Sprint GTs and their derivatives may find the following list of specialists useful. They are not Alfa main dealers, since franchises frequently change hands, and there rarely any heritage memory. Most of the companies listed here have been Alfa Romeo specialists for some time. But for a fuller and up to date listing, check with the Owners' Club. There are some interesting websites around, including www.aroc-uk.com, www. mgscoachworks.com and www.alfaclassifieds.com, which have links to other sites. Please note that the inclusion of a specialist in the following list is not necessarily a guarantee of good service, and that neither publisher nor author can accept any responsibility for any problems you may encounter with these independent companies.

Alfa II, Ramesh Bharadia, Unit 5, Parr Road, Stanmore, HA7 1NL, UK. Tel: 0208 951 4100.
(Alfa servicing, sales from *1970* onwards, exchange engines).

AC Trofeo Motorsport, Nigel Cottee or Alan Marshall, Unit 11, Churchfield Court Top Valley, Bewcastle Road, Nottingham, NO5 9PJ, UK. Tel: 01159 204211.

AFRA SAS, Snra. Croci, Via Carducci 36, 20019 Settimo Milanese, Italy, Tel: 0039 02 3286111.
(Rare Alfa Romeo spares, ex-factory or made to order).

Alfa Parts Exchange, Larry Dickman, 2000 National Avenue, Hayward, CA 94545, USA, Tel: 001 510 782 5800.
(Used components, 1950-1994 US-spec cars)

Alfa Ricambi, Julius T. Mann or Brad L. Bunch, 6644 San Fernando Road, Glendale, CA 91201, USA, Tel: 001 818 956 7933.

Alfa Romeo Giulia 105 Register, Stuart Taylor, 144 Sussex Way, Cockfosters, Barnet, Herts, EN4 0BG, UK.

Alfa Romeo Giulietta Register, Peter Shaw, Grange Farm House, 2, Bedford Road, Willington, Beds, MK44 3PS, UK.

Alfa Romeo Owners' Club, Secretary: Ken Carrington, 40 Maltings Road, Great Baddow, Chelmsford, Essex, UK, Tel: 01245 473455.

Alfa Romeo Championship Association, Secretary: Michael Lindsay, 97 High Street, Linton, Cambridge, CB1 6JT, UK, Tel: 01223 894300.
(Alfa Romeo race series)

Alfashop Ltd, Jeremy Wales, Unit 1 Beech Drive, Mile Cross Lane, Norwich, NR6 6RN, UK, Tel: 01603 426277.
(Importer of spare parts).

Alfa Romeo Owners' Club Shop, Ray Skilling, EM Models, 42 Camden Road, Tunbridge Wells, Kent, TN1 2QD, UK, Tel: 01892 536689

Alfatune, Gus Lambrou, Merton Bank Road, St Helens, Merseyside, WA9 1HP, UK, Tel: 01744 25499.
(Road, race and rally preparation).

Alfa Servizio, Colin Wing, Unit 79, Bunting Road Industrial Estate, Northampton, NN2 6EE, UK.

Arese T.H.O., Ing. C.J. Violier, Leeweg 7, 1161AA Zwanenburg, Netherlands, Tel: 0031 543451906.
(Parts, repairs, tuning).

Alfaholics, Richard Banks, Oakford, Tiverton, Devon, UK, Tel: 01398 351360.
(Classic Alfa sales, components specialists).

See also:
Richard Norris, 44A The Gardens, East Dulwich, London, SE22 9QQ, UK.
Tel: 0208 299 2929.

Alfa Stop, Tony Stevens, PO   Box 50, Belper, Derbyshire, DE56 1AS, UK, Tel: 0177 382 2000.
(Classic Alfa brake, clutch, transmission and exhaust systems specialist, 1950 - 1966).

Ken Bell, St James's Road, Fleet, Hants, GU13 9QR, UK, Tel: 01252 629159.
(Service, repairs).

Bell and Colvill, Bobby Bell or Martin Colvill, Epsom Road, West Horsley, Surrey, KT24 6DG, UK, Tel: 014865 4671.
(Alfa Romeo specialists).

Alfarama, Westmoreland Road, London, NW9 9RL, UK, Tel: 0207 206 2075.

Automeo, Les Dufty, 36 Gypsy Patch Lane, Little Stoke, Bristol, UK, Tel: 0117 969 5771.
(Alfa Romeo servicing, spares, maintenance, carburettor specialist).

155

Benalfa Cars, Alan Bennett, 19 Washington Road, West Wilts Trading Estate, Westbury, Wiltshire, UK, Tel: 01373 864333.
(Alfa Romeo restorations, engine rebuilds).

BLS Automotive, Tom Shrubb or Phil Bower, Unit 1 Great Northern Way, Lincoln, LNS 8XF, UK.
(Dealership, plus race preparation).

The Carburettor Hospital, Eric Archer or James Cooper, 210 Wood Grange Drive, Southend-on-Sea, Essex, SS1 2SJ, UK.
(UK's largest carburettor stockist).

Classic Alfas, Ian Williams, Camden Garage, 9 Camden Terrace, Weston-super-Mare, Somerset, BS23 3DH, UK.
(Service and MoT checks, parts sourcing for Giulietta models).

Classic Car Interiors, Chris Adams, Park Farmhouse, Cornworthy, Totnes, Devon, TQ9 7ES, UK, Tel: 01803 732454.
(Original pre-1976 Alfa Romeo upholstery).

Cloverleaf Transmissions, Charlie Skinner, 70 Millet Avenue, Harleston, London, W10 8AP, UK, Tel: 0208 961 2355.
(Mechanical, transmission overhauls).

T.A. & J.M. Coburn, Widhill House, Blunsdon, Swindon, Wilts, UK, Tel: 01793 721501.
(Alfa Romeo upholstery specialist).

C.P. Garage Services, Euan Colbron, Unit 3 Blauniefield Industrial Estate, Dundee, DD4 8UT, Scotland, Tel: 01382 731479.
(Servicing and parts).

Cubleys of Ainsdale, Mike Haliday, 609 Liverpool Road, Southport, Merseyside, PR8 3NG, UK.
(Alfa dealer, new and used spares).

Bob Dove Motorsport, 71 Celeborn Street, South Woodham Ferrers, Essex, CM3 7AF, UK, Tel: 01245 328278.
(Race preparation, bits and pieces).

Richard Drake Motors, Unit 2, Renson Close, Beech Drive, Mile Cross Lane, Norwich, NR6 6RH, UK, Tel: 01603 406050.

(Alfa Romeo servicing, engine rebuilds, race preparation).

DRH Developments, Dave Hood, 20 Daventry Road, Dunchurch, Warwickshire, CV22 6NS, UK, Tel: 01788 815936.
(Race preparation, mechanical and electrical work).

Duetto Tuning, Willem van Voorthuyzen, Haarlemmer Houttuinen 17-19, 1013 GL Amsterdam, Netherlands, Tel: 0031 20627 6969.
(105-Series engine specialist, particularly GTAs).

E.B. Spares (The Italian Connection), David Edgington or Kevin Abigail, 31 Link Road, Westbury Trading Estate, Westbury, Wilts, BA13 4JB, UK, Tel: 01373 823856.
(Parts specialists: www.ebspares.co.uk).

Jim Evans, Scagglethorpe Manor, Malton, North Yorkshire, YO17 8DT, UK, Tel: 01944 758909.
(Race preparation of 105-Series engines and suspension).

Excellent Bodyshop Ltd, Nino di Luca, 8 Johnson's Way, Park Royal, London, NW10 7QB, UK, Tel: 0181 453 0282.
(Restoration and bodywork repairs).

Frenitalia TarOx, R. Cappucci, Unit 9, Taylor Court, Carr's Industrial Estate, Haslingden, BB4 5LA, Lancs, UK, Tel: 01706 222872.
(UK importer of TarOx brake systems).

Gatwick Alfa, Mike Buckler, Rusper Garage, High Street, Rusper, Horsham, West Sussex, RH12 4PX, UK, Tel: 01293 871155.
(Spares and repairs, 1950s to 1990s, race preparation).

John Goodchild Motor Engineers, 112 Turnpike Link, Croydon, CR0 5NY, UK, Tel: 0208 680 2120.
(Repairs, servicing, maintenance, especially 105-Series cars).

P. D. Gough & Co, The Old Foundry, Common Lane, Whatnall, Nottingham, NG16 1HD, UK, Tel: 01159 382241.
(Hand-built stainless steel exhaust systems).

Gran Turismo Engineering, Simon Whiting, Station Avenue, Kew Gardens, Surrey, UK, Tel 0207 460 0007.
(Classic Alfa Romeo specialist, sales race preparation).

Harvey Bailey Engineering Ltd, Anne Harvey Bailey, Ladycroft Farm, Kniveton, Ashboume, Derby, DE6 1JH, UK, Tel: 01335 346419.
(Suspension tuning experts).

High Performance Restorations, Robert Thompson, Oak Farm, Wilcot Lane, Nesscliff, Shrewsbury, Shropshire, SY4 1DB, UK, Tel: 01743 741592.
(Bead-blasting and powder-coating specialst).

Italian Miniatures, Richard Crompton, 39 Penncricket Lane, Oldbury, Warley, West Midlands, B68 8LX, UK, Tel: 0121 559 6611.
(Alfa Romeo scale models).

The Highwood Motor Company, Chris Sweetapple, 137, Bishopston Road, Swansea, SA3 3EX, Wales, Tel: 01792 234314.
(Alfa Romeo replacement panels and components specialist; workshop manuals on CD ROM).

Peter E. Hilliard & Son, 41 High Street, Penge, London, SE20 7HJ, UK, Tel: 0181 778 5755.
(Servicing and repairs, all Alfas from 1963).

Lombarda Carriage Company, Colin Fallon or Mark Wakeford, 3-10 Railway Mews, London, W10 6HN, UK, Tel: 0207 2430638.
(Alfa spares and sales).

K & L Autos, Keith Waite, Golders Green, London, N5, UK, Tel: 0208 4583879 or 0585 655503.
(Mobile servicing of classic Alfas).

London Stainless, Giles Beaumont or Paul Goddard, 251 Queenstown Road, Battersea, London, SWB 3NP, UK, Tel: 0207 622 2120.
(Stainless-steel exhaust systems for virtually all post-war Alfas, mail order).

Lyles of Newcastle Ltd, Jason Sanderson or Ian Dodsworth, Milano House, West Road, Newcastle-upon-Tyne, NE15 6PQ, UK, Tel: 0191 2730700.
(Sales, parts and service).

Alwyn Kershaw, Peter Colley, Langford Garage, Helmsley, York, YO4 1NF, England, Tel: 01759 373399.
(Alfa dealers, special tuning).

Mangoletsi, Knutsford, Cheshire, England, Tel: 01565 722899.

(Alfa sales, service, parts).

MGS Coachworks, Mike Spenceley, 2 Foxley Hill Road, Purley, Surrey, CR8 2HB, UK, Tel: 0208 645 0555.
(Alfa restoration experts).

MP Racing, Piero Pesaro, Unit C, Davis Road, Chessington, Surrey, KT9 1TI, UK, Tel: 0208 974 1749.
(Performance tuning of older Alfas).

R. Proietti Ltd, Stef or Bruno, 2 Blundell Street, London, N7 9BJ, UK, Tel: 0207 6070798.
(Maintenance of Alfas of all ages).

Brian Pillans, 129 Maxwell Drive, Glasgow, GH1 5AE, Scotland, Tel: 0141 3313424.
(New and used parts for post-1965 Alfas).

Jamie Porter, Rowland House, Lower Gower Road, Royston, Herts, UK, Tel: 01920 822987.
(Alfa servicing, spares, rolling road, maintenance).

Ramponi Rockell, Alex Jenkins, 30-31 Lancaster Mews, London, W2 3QE, UK, Tel: 0207 262 7383.
(Alfa Romeo sales, servicing).

Sunnyside Garage, David Lai, Unit L5, Chadwell Heath Industrial Park, Kemp Road, Dagenham, Essex, RM8 1SL, England.
(Mechanical & electrical repairs)

Julius Thurgood, Broomfield Farm, Coleshill Road, Bentley, Warwicks, CV9 2JS, UK, Tel: 01827 720361.
(Organiser: Top Hat and Alfa GTA Challenge race series).

Premier Garage, Rob Kirby, High Street, Newport, Essex, CB11 3PE, England, Tel: 01799 541041.
(Service, repairs, tuning, etc.).

Rossi Engineering, Rob Giordanelli, Sunbury on Thames, Surrey, England, Tel: 01932 786819.
(Race preparation, restoration, maintenance).

Prinz Bredevoort, Henk Prinz, Kleine Gracht 10, 7126 AW Bredevoort, Netherlands.
(Parts for 105-Series cars).

Timeless Motor Company, John Timpany, Pooles Lane, Highwood, Chelmsford, Essex, UK, Tel: 01245 248008.
(Overhauls, repairs, restorations, especially 105-series).

Spider's Web, Roger Longmate, Westgate Street, Hilborough, Thetford, Norfolk, IP26 5BN, UK, Tel: 01760 756229.
(Rebuilds and restorations).

Touring Superleggera, Andrew Thorogood, 172 Clapham Park Road, London, SW4 7DU, England, Tel: 0207 720 8616.
(Classic Alfa restoration, race preparation).

Fa. Tuynder C.V., J. Tuynder, Westvlietweg 40, 2267 AB Leidschendam, Netherlands, Tel: 0031 703874403.
(Parts by mail order).

Veloce Cars, Romford, Essex, England, Tel: 0208 551 0644.
(Secondhand Alfa sales, spares).

Veloce Sport, Adam Andrews, Pine Warren Boston Road, Heckington, Nr. Sleaford, Lincs, NO34 9JF, England, Tel: 08707 583563.
(Car sales and parts from 1968 to 1998).

Westbury Insurance Services, 23 Castle Street, High Wycombe, Bucks, HP13 6RU, England, Tel: 01494 444574.
(Alfa Romeo insurance specialist).

Westune Auto Services, Peter or Simon West, Marsh Street, Horwich, Bolton, Lancs, BL6 7TA, England, Tel: 01204 697535.
(Servicing, tuning, etc.).

John Williams Classics, Unit B, Little Park Farm, Abbotts Ann, Near Andover, Hampshire, SP11 7AU, England, Tel: (sales/service) 01264 711003, Web: www. johnwilliamsclassiccars.com.
(Sales, servicing and restoration of classic Alfa Romeos and Lancias).

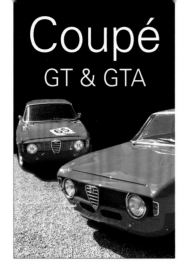

Coupé
GT & GTA

Appendix 5

Alfa Romeo Giulia Coupé Contemporary Road Tests

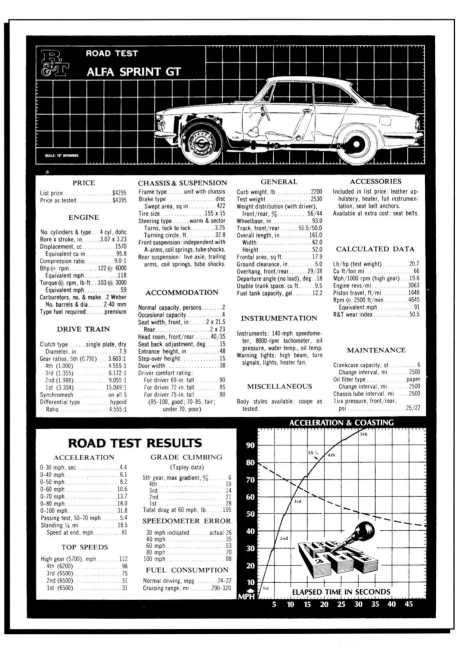

ROAD TEST
ALFA SPRINT GT

SCALE: 10" DIVISIONS

PRICE

List price $4295
Price as tested $4395

ENGINE

No. cylinders & type .. 4 cyl, dohc
Bore x stroke, in....... 3.07 x 3.23
Displacement, cc........... 1570
    Equivalent cu in 95.8
Compression ratio 9.0:1
Bhp @ rpm.......... 122 @ 6000
    Equivalent mph........... 118
Torque @ rpm, lb-ft .. 103 @ 3000
    Equivalent mph........... 59
Carburetors, no. & make .. 2 Weber
    No. barrels & dia........ 2-40 mm
Type fuel required....... premium

DRIVE TRAIN

Clutch type...... single plate, dry
    Diameter, in 7.9
Gear ratios, 5th (0.791) .. 3.603:1
    4th (1.000) 4.555:1
    3rd (1.355) 6.172:1
    2nd (1.988) 9.055:1
    1st (3.304) 15.049:1
Synchromesh .... on all 5
Differential type......... hypoid
    Ratio................. 4.555:1

CHASSIS & SUSPENSION

Frame type...... unit with chassis
Brake type.................. disc
    Swept area, sq in 422
Tire size............... 155 x 15
Steering type...... worm & sector
    Turns, lock to lock 3.25
    Turning circle, ft........ 32.8
Front suspension: independent with
    A-arms, coil springs, tube shocks.
Rear suspension: live axle, trailing
    arms, coil springs, tube shocks.

ACCOMMODATION

Normal capacity, persons........ 2
Occasional capacity 4
Seat width, front, in ...... 2 x 21.5
    Rear .... 2 x 23
Head room, front/rear..... 40/35
Seat back adjustment, deg..... 15
Entrance height, in.......... 48
Step-over height 15
Door width 38
Driver comfort rating:
    For driver 69-in. tall........ 90
    For driver 72-in. tall........ 85
    For driver 75-in. tall........ 80
    (85-100, good; 70-85, fair;
        under 70, poor)

GENERAL

Curb weight, lb............ 2200
Test weight 2530
Weight distribution (with driver),
    front/rear, %.......... 56/44
Wheelbase, in.............. 93.0
Track, front/rear 51.5/50.0
Overall length, in 161.0
    Width 62.0
    Height 52.0
Frontal area, sq ft.......... 17.9
Ground clearance, in......... 5.0
Overhang, front/rear....... 29/38
Departure angle (no load), deg .18
Usable trunk space, cu ft..... 9.5
Fuel tank capacity, gal...... 12.2

INSTRUMENTATION

Instruments: 140-mph speedometer, 8000-rpm tachometer, oil pressure, water temp., oil temp.
Warning lights: high beam, turn signals, lights, heater fan.

MISCELLANEOUS

Body styles available: coupe as tested.

ACCESSORIES

Included in list price: leather up-holstery, heater, full instrumentation, seat belt anchors.
Available at extra cost: seat belts.

CALCULATED DATA

Lb/hp (test weight).......... 20.7
Cu ft/ton mi 66
Mph/1000 rpm (high gear)... 19.6
Engine revs/mi............. 3063
Piston travel, ft/mi......... 1648
Rpm @ 2500 ft/min........ 4645
    Equivalent mph........... 91
R&T wear index............ 50.5

MAINTENANCE

Crankcase capacity, qt.......... 6
    Change interval, mi....... 2500
Oil filter type.............. paper
    Change interval, mi....... 2500
Chassis lube interval, mi..... 2500
Tire pressure, front/rear,
    psi................... 25/27

ROAD TEST RESULTS

ACCELERATION

0-30 mph, sec	4.4
0-40 mph.................	6.1
0-50 mph.................	8.2
0-60 mph.................	10.6
0-70 mph.................	13.7
0-80 mph.................	18.0
0-100 mph	31.8
Passing test, 50-70 mph.....	5.4
Standing ¼ mi	18.5
Speed at end, mph..........	81

TOP SPEEDS

High gear (5700), mph....	112
4th (6200)	96
3rd (6500)	75
2nd (6500)	51
1st (6500)	31

GRADE CLIMBING
(Tapley data)

5th gear, max gradient, %	6
4th	10
3rd	14
2nd	21
1st	28
Total drag at 60 mph, lb.....	105

SPEEDOMETER ERROR

30 mph indicated	.... actual	26
40 mph	....	35
60 mph	....	53
80 mph	....	70
100 mph	....	88

FUEL CONSUMPTION

Normal driving, mpg	24-27
Cruising range, mi ...	290-320

ACCELERATION & COASTING

ELAPSED TIME IN SECONDS

Road & Track's road test data panel from their report on the Alfa Sprint GT 1600 dated December 1964. R&T concluded " ...for those people who doubt that racing improves the breed, the characteristics of the Alfa Romeo Giulia Sprint GT would seem to prove conclusively that it does."

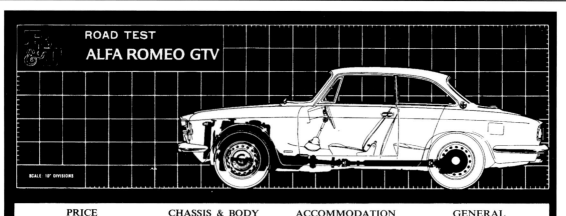

PRICE

Basic list. $4200
As tested $4448

ENGINE

Type . . . . 4 cyl inline, dohc
Bore x stroke, mm . . . . 78 x 82
  Equivalent in . . . . . 3.07 x 3.23
Displacement, cc cu in . .1570 95.8
Compression ratio 9.0:1
Bhp @ rpm . . . . 125 @ 6000
  Equivalent mph 116
Torque @ rpm, lb-ft . 115 @ 2800
  Equivalent mph 54
Carburetion . 2 Weber 40 DCOE 27
Type fuel required . . . . . premium

DRIVE TRAIN

Clutch diameter, in 7.9
Gear ratios: 5th (0.79) . . . 3.60:1
  4th (1.00) 4.56:1
  3rd (1.36) 6.21:1
  2nd (1.99) 9.08:1
  1st (3.30) 15.0:1
Synchromesh . . . . on all 5
Final drive ratio 4.56:1

CHASSIS & BODY

Body/frame. . . . . steel unit
Brake type: ATE disc with vacuum
  assist, drum parking brake
  Swept area, sq in 368
Wheel type & size, in . . . .15 x 4.5
Tires . . Pirelli Cinturato S 155-15
Steering type . . . . . worm & sector
  Overall ratio 15:1
  Turns, lock-to-lock 3.75
  Turning circle, ft 32.8
Front suspension: independent with
  unequal-length A-arms, coil
  springs, tube shocks, anti-roll bar.
Rear suspension: live axle, trailing
  arms, coil springs, tube shocks.

OPTIONAL EQUIPMENT

Included in "as tested" price: AM/
FM SW radio, 2 seat & shoulder
belts, outside mirror.
Other: cast alloy wheels, rear seat
belts, rear window defroster.

ACCOMMODATION

Seating capacity, persons . .2 + 2
Seat width, front/rear
         . . . . . .2 x 21.5/2x23.0
Head room, front/rear . 40.0/35.0
Seat back adjustment, deg . . . 30
Driver comfort rating (scale of 100):
  Driver 69 in. tall. 85
  Driver 72 in. tall. 80
  Driver 75 in. tall 75

INSTRUMENTATION

Instruments: 140-mph speedometer, 8000-rpm tachometer; oil
pressure, oil temp, water temp
& fuel level gauges.
Warning lights: generator, direc-
tional signals, lights on, high
beam, heater on, low fuel.

MAINTENANCE

Crankcase capacity, qt 6.0
  Change interval, mi 3600
Filter change interval, mi . . . 3600
Chassis lube interval, mi . . . 3600
Tire pressures, psi 24,26

MISCELLANEOUS

Body styles available: coupe as
tested.
Warranty period, 6 mo/unlimited
mileage.

GENERAL

Curb weight, lb 2230
Test weight 2625
Weight distribution (with
  driver), front/rear, % 53/47
Wheelbase, in 93.0
Track, front/rear 51.5/50.0
Overall length 161.0
  Width 62.0
  Height 52.0
Frontal area, sq ft 17.9
Ground clearance, in 5.0
Overhang, front/rear . .30.4/37.6
Usable trunk space, cu ft . . . 9.5
Fuel tank capacity, gal 14.0

CALCULATED DATA

Lb/hp (test wt) 21.0
Mph/1000 rpm (5th gear) . . . 19.6
Engine revs/mi (60 mph) . . . 3060
Piston travel, ft/mi 1645
Rpm @ 2500 ft/min 4645
  Equivalent mph 91
Cu ft/ton mi 64.4
R&T wear index 50.4
Brake swept area sq in/ton 280

ROAD TEST RESULTS

ACCELERATION

Time to distance, sec:
  0-100 ft 3.7
  0-250 ft 6.3
  0-500 ft 9.6
  0-750 ft 12.5
  0-1000 ft 14.9
  0-1320 ft (¼ mi) 17.6
Speed at end of ¼ mi, mph . . 77
Time to speed, sec:
  0-30 mph 3.4
  0-40 mph 5.5
  0-50 mph 7.2
  0-60 mph 10.5
  0-70 mph 14.2
  0-80 mph 19.2
  0-100 mph 35.5
Passing exposure time, sec:
  To pass car going 50 mph . .7.4

FUEL CONSUMPTION

Normal driving, mpg 21-25
Cruising range, mi 295-350

SPEEDS IN GEARS

5th gear (5700 rpm), mph 112
  4th (6800) 104
  3rd (6800) 77
  2nd (6800) 53
  1st (6800) 31

BRAKES

Panic stop from 80 mph:
  Deceleration, % g 78
  Control . . . . excellent
Fade test: percent of increase in
  pedal effort required to maintain
  50%-g deceleration rate in six
  stops from 60 mph 11
Parking brake: hold 30% grade . .no
Overall brake rating . . . very good

SPEEDOMETER ERROR

30 mph indicated . . . . actual 26.8
40 mph 36.0
60 mph 54.6
80 mph 73.2
100 mph 91.4
Odometer, 10.0 mi . . . . actual 9.62

ACCELERATION & COASTING

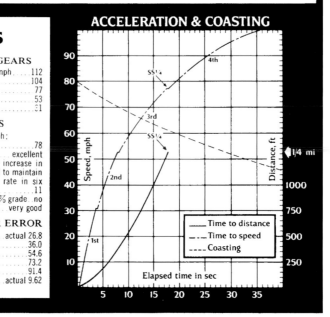

Time to distance
Time to speed
Coasting

Elapsed time in sec

Opposite: In its July 1967 test of the 1600 GTV, Road & Track *said in conclusion "The combination of light, precise steering and controllable understeer through almost any road condition makes it an easy, safe and enjoyable car for the novice, as well as a source of continuing exhilaration to the skilled driver." Here is the data panel from that test.*

Motor *magazine road tested the 1750 GTV in an article entitled "Flair for speed" dated July 13th, 1968. Their overall assessment of the car was "Stylish high performance two-door coupé with superb handling and roadholding; economy excellent."* Motor's *road test data is reproduced here.*

Performance

Conditions

Weather: Warm and dry, wind 5 m.p.h.
Temperature approx. 65°F.
Surface: Dry tarmacadam.
Fuel: 98 octane (RM). 4-star rating.

Maximum speeds

	m.p.h.	k.p.h.
Mean opposite runs	115.5	185.5
Best one-way kilometre	118.0	189.9
4th gear	107.0	172.0
3rd gear	80.0	129.0
2nd gear	54.0	87.0
1st gear	33.0	53.0

"Maximile" speed: (Timed quarter mile after 1 mile accelerating from rest)

Mean	109.7 m.p.h.
Best	112.3 m.p.h.

Acceleration times

m.p.h.	sec.
0-30	3.0
0-40	4.8
0-50	6.8
0-60	9.3
0-70	12.7
0-80	16.7
0-90	22.3
0-100	29.7

m.p.h.	5th sec.	4th sec.	3rd sec.
10-30	—·	—	6.8
20-40	13.6	8.6	5.7
30-50	13.2	8.1	5.8
40-60	11.1	7.5	5.5
50-70	11.5	8.0	6.1
60-80	13.3	9.0	6.8
70-90	17.0	10.0	—

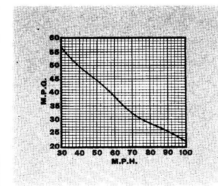

Fuel consumption

Touring (consumption midway between 30 m.p.h. and maximum less 5% allowance for acceleration) . . . . 29.5 m.p.g.
Overall . . . . 23.4 m.p.g.
(=12.1 litres/100km)
Total test distance . . . . 1,713 miles

Brakes

Pedal pressure, deceleration and equivalent stopping distance from 30 m.p.h.

lb.	g	ft.
25	0.48	62½
50	1.02	29
Handbrake	0.30	100

Fade test

20 stops at ½g deceleration at 1 min. intervals from a speed midway between 40 m.p.h. and maximum speed (=78 m.p.h.)

	lb.
Pedal force at beginning	25
Pedal force at 10th stop	25
Pedal force at 20th stop	25

Steering

Turning circle between kerbs: ft.
Left 36¾
Right 34½
Turns of steering wheel from lock to lock . . 3½
Steering wheel deflection for 50 ft. diameter circle . . . . 1 turn

Clutch

Free pedal movement . . . . = 1 in.
Additional movement to disengage clutch completely . . . . = 4 in.
Maximum pedal load . . . . =42 lb.

Speedometer

Indicated	30	40	50	60	70
True	27½	37	47½	57½	67
Indicated		80	90	100	110
True		76	85	93	102

Distance recorder . . . . 3.5% fast

Weight

Kerb weight (unladen with fuel for approximately 50 miles) . . . . 20.0 cwt.
Front/rear distribution 57/43
Weight laden as tested . . . . 23.8 cwt.

Parkability

Gap needed to clear 6ft wide obstruction parked in front:

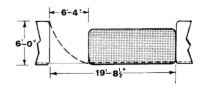

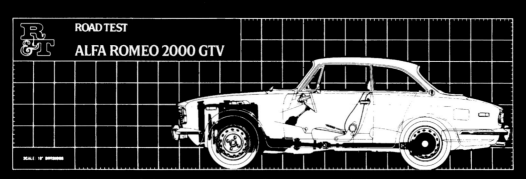

ROAD TEST
ALFA ROMEO 2000 GTV

SCALE: 18" REPRESENTS

PRICE

List price, East/Gulf Coast ... $5249
List price, West Coast ... $5299
Price as tested:
West Coast ... $5464
Price as tested includes standard equipment (4-wheel disc brakes, fuel injection, 5-speed transmission), limited-slip diff ($115), dealer prep ($50).

IMPORTER

Alfa-Romeo, Inc.
250 Sylvan Ave.,
Englewood Cliffs, New Jersey 08732

ENGINE

Type ... dohc inline 4
Bore x stroke, mm ... 84.0 x 88.5
Equivalent in ... 3.31 x 3.48
Displacement, cc/cu in ... 1962/120
Compression ratio ... 9.0:1
Bhp @ rpm, net ... 129 @ 5800
Equivalent mph ... 112
Torque @ rpm, lb-ft ... 132 @ 3500
Equivalent mph ... 68
Fuel Injection ... Alfa-Spica mech
Fuel requirement ... regular, 91-oct
Emissions, gram/mile:
Hydrocarbons ... 2.00
Carbon Monoxide ... 16.2
Nitrogen Oxides ... 1.53

DRIVE TRAIN

Transmission ... 5-speed manual
Gear ratios: (0.79) ... 3.60:1
4th (1.00) ... 4.56:1
3rd (1.35) ... 6.16:1
2nd (1.99) ... 9.07:1
1st (3.30) ... 15.05:1
Final drive ratio ... 4.56:1

CHASSIS & BODY

Layout ... front engine/rear drive
Body/frame ... unit steel
Brake system ... 10.7-in disc front, 10.5-in. disc rear; vacuum assisted
Swept area, sq in ... 397
Wheels ... steel disc 14 x 5½
Tires ... Pirelli Cinturato 165HR-14
Steering type ... recirculating ball
Turns, lock-to-lock ... 3.8
Turning circle, ft ... 34.8
Front suspension: unequal-length A-arms, coil springs, tube shocks, anti-roll bar
Rear suspension: live axle on trailing arms & upper transverse-trailing link; coil springs, tube shocks, anti-roll bar

ACCOMMODATION

Seating capacity, persons ... 2+2
Seat width, front/rear ... 19.0/19.0
Head room, front/rear ... 36.0/34.0
Seat back adjustment, degrees ... 50

INSTRUMENTATION

Instruments: 140-mph speedometer, 8000-rpm tachometer, 99,999 odometer, 999.9 trip odometer, oil pressure, coolant temperature, fuel level
Warning lights: brake system, alternator, oil level, fuel pressure, throttle, heater blower, lights on, high beam, directionals, seat belts

MAINTENANCE

Service intervals, mi:
Oil change ... 3000
Filter change ... 3000
Chassis lube ... 3000
Minor tuneup ... 6000
Major tuneup ... 12,000
Warranty, mo/mi ... 6/unlimited

GENERAL

Curb weight, lb ... 2325
Test weight ... 2660
Weight distribution (with driver), front/rear, % ... 56/44
Wheelbase, in ... 92.5
Track, front/rear ... 52.1/50.1
Length ... 161.4
Width ... 62.2
Height ... 51.8
Ground clearance ... 5.0
Overhang, front/rear ... 29.4/39.5
Usable trunk space, cu ft ... 8.7
Fuel capacity, U.S. gal ... 14.0

CALCULATED DATA

Lb/bhp (test weight) ... 20.6
Mph/1000 rpm (5th gear) ... 19.0
Engine revs/mi (60 mph) ... 3550
Piston travel, ft/mi ... 2060
R&T steering index ... 1.32
Brake swept area, sq in/ton ... 299

RELIABILITY

From R&T Owner Surveys the average number of trouble areas for all models surveyed is 11. As owners of earlier-model Alfa Romeos reported 11 trouble areas, we expect the reliability of the Alfa Romeo 2000 GTV to be average.

ACCELERATION

Time to distance, sec:
0-100 ft ... 4.5
0-500 ft ... 9.8
0-1320 ft (¼ mi) ... 17.6
Speed at end of ¼-mi, mph ... 80.5
Time to speed, sec:
0-30 mph ... 3.3
0-40 mph ... 4.7
0-50 mph ... 6.8
0-60 mph ... 9.6
0-70 mph ... 13.1
0-80 mph ... 17.3
0-90 mph ... 23.3

SPEEDS IN GEARS

5th gear (5800 rpm) ... 110
4th (5800) ... 89
3rd (5800) ... 66
2nd (5800) ... 45
1st (5800) ... 27

SPEEDOMETER ERROR

30 mph indicated is actually ... 27.0
50 mph ... 46.0
60 mph ... 55.0
70 mph ... 65.0
80 mph ... 74.0
Odometer, 10.0 mi ... 9.5

BRAKES

Minimum stopping distances, ft:
From 60 mph ... 150
From 80 mph ... 287
Control in panic stop ... good
Pedal effort for 0.5g stop, lb ... 13
Fade: percent increase in pedal effort to maintain 0.5g deceleration in 6 stops from 60 mph ... nil
Parking: hold 30% grade? ... yes
Overall brake rating ... good

HANDLING

Speed on 100-ft radius, mph ... 32.7
Lateral acceleration, g ... 0.715

FUEL ECONOMY

Normal driving, mpg ... 23.8
Cruising range, mi (1-gal res.) ... 309

INTERIOR NOISE

All noise readings in dBA:
Idle in neutral ... 56
Maximum, 1st gear ... 85
Constant 30 mph (4th gear) ... 68
50 mph (5th gear) ... 71
70 mph ... 78
90 mph ... 86

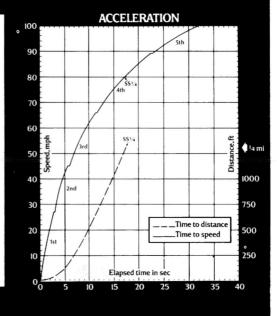

ACCELERATION

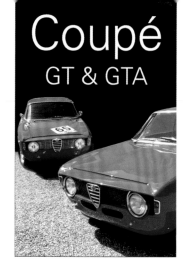

Coupé
GT & GTA

Appendix 6

**Radford
Alfa Romeo
Giulia
Sprint GT**

Harold Radford (Coachbuilders)
Limited would rebuild a Gulia
coupé to a very high specification,
installing luxury trim and equipment.
Rectangular Cibié headlights were
an instant giveaway. Over this and
the following three pages, Radford's
contemporary sales brochure is
reproduced.

RADFORD

*Alfa Romeo
Giulia
Sprint GT*

*When you
want to be
really different –
It's attention
to detail
that counts*

Opposite: When Road & Track road
tested the Alfa 2000 GTV in August
1972 it talked about "an old friend"
with detail improvements and a bigger
engine. Generally, it felt the car was
showing its age and had to conclude
- "The GTV is a good 1964 design,
overdue for a change. Don't get us
wrong; the 2000 GTV is still a good
car and a capable performer ..." R&T's
data panel is reproduced here.

Ever wondered what makes a car different — really different? It's attention to detail. The sort of details which make the real difference between travelling in comfort and nearly travelling in comfort.
The sort of attention to detail which ensures that everything is where it ought to be, and that everything is on the car when you buy it. The sort of detail that shows that someone wanted you to be absolutely contented with your motor car. The sort of detail which says 'luxury and quality' in any language.

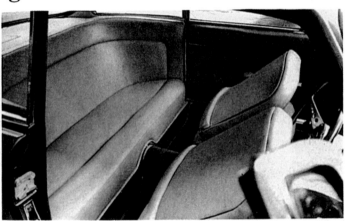

The Radford version of the Alfa Romeo Giulia Sprint GT is a *really* different motor car. Harold Radford (Coachbuilders) Limited have transformed the Giulia Sprint GT by attention to detail.

New colours – for the fastidious, Radford have selected a range of fascinating colours, sprayed with all the coachbuilder's traditional care to make the Radford version of the Giulia Sprint GT *really* different.

New style – from the front to the back, Radford's attention to detail has smoothed the lines of an already basically beautiful motor car. New anodised aluminium grille with recessed rectangular headlamps at the front look good, provide safe lighting for after-dark fast motoring. Stylish recessed panel with stainless

steel surround at rear, stainless steel gravel rails sweep along each side of the car to make it *really* different. Inside – the interior of the Radford-converted Giulia Sprint GT is a revelation of ultimate good taste, and supreme luxury. What is not so immediately obvious is the meticulous attention to the convenience and safety of driver and passengers. Contoured seating for the driver and front seat passenger ensures that you can drive a very long way indeed without feeling any fatigue. In the back, an exclusive 'Cleopatra' couch allows two adult passengers to travel in comfort, two children to motor in luxury. All seats are upholstered in breathing cirrus material or leather, which maintains a constant temperature

under all conditions, allows you to travel comfortably, arrive refreshed. This material, easily cleaned and very hard wearing, will never sag or crease. A completely re-designed fascia is fully instrumented and faced with rosewood. Matt black instrument area permits instant scanning of the dials. Controls for the (optional) electrically operated window lifts and the radio are placed readily to hand on the centre console. Doors luxuriously trimmed in cirrus material with walnut cappings and carpeted kick shields. Automatic warning lights on door trailing edges warn other drivers whenever a door is opened. Thick pile carpeting covering the entire floor area completes an interior which is *really* different.

RADFORD Alfa Romeo Giulia Sprint GT

Photographs: Stephano Archetti

Thanks to extensive soundproofing you will seldom hear the zippy 1570 c.c. Alfa Romeo engine – but lift the bonnet and you can see that it's still there! Capable of giving traditional Alfa Romeo performance throughout its range – purring through traffic, whispering up the motorway. Roadholding is naturally impeccable, and the Radford-converted Giulia GT does not cost the earth to run.

Do not let mere description sway your judgement – test drive the Radford version of the Alfa Romeo Giulia Sprint GT, and feel what it's like to drive a motor car which is *really* different.

Harold Radford (Coachbuilders) build luxury and quality into the Giulia Sprint GT with the following items as standard equipment: redesigned padded fascia; centre console with radio, heater controls, cigar lighter and ashtray; Microcell

front seats trimmed in Freudenberg PVC; one-piece 'Cleopatra' rear seat; Cibie rectangular headlights set into special grille with air vents below; deep-pile carpeting; coachbuilder's exterior finish with fine-line motif and gravel rails; reversing light; door warning lights; full sound deadening treatment. For further luxury a wide range of optional equipment is available, including: electrically-operated window lifts; leather upholstery; record player; tape recorder; electrically-operated radio aerial; full air conditioning. Thanks to Radford's experience of building motor cars which are *really* different, the company is prepared to undertake the installation of any item of luxury equipment (within reason) specified by clients ordering the Radford version of the Alfa Romeo Giulia Sprint GT.

Brief specification
Engine – 4-cylinder, in line, bore 78 mm., stroke 82 mm., capacity 1570 c.c. Gross B.H.P. 122 at 6000 r.p.m. Two horizontal, twin-choke carburettors. Twin overhead camshafts.
Transmission – SDP clutch, five forward speeds and reverse. Synchromesh on all forward gears. Floor-mounted gear shift. Live rear axle with hypoid final drive.
Suspension – I.F.S. by inclined transverse wishbones with anti-roll bar, and coil spring/damper units. Rear axle located by coil spring/damper units, with longitudinal torque arms and rubber bushes.
Steering – Re-circulating ball or worm and roller.
Brakes – All-disc, hydraulically-operated with vacuum servo. Hand brake mechanically operates on rear brakes.

HAROLD RADFORD (COACHBUILDERS) LIMITED 124 KING STREET HAMMERSMITH LONDON W6 RIVERSIDE 8831

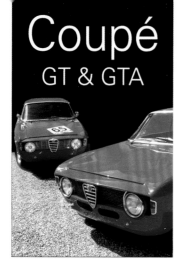

Coupé
GT & GTA

Appendix 7

GTA
Sample
Homologation
Papers

AUTOMOBILE CLUB D'ITALIA
COMMISSIONE SPORTIVA AUTOMOBILISTICA ITALIANA
FEDERATION INTERNATIONALE DE L'AUTOMOBILE

Scheda di Omologazione
secondo l'allegato **J** al Codice Sportivo Internazionale

Casa costruttrice ......ALFA ROMEO........................ Modello ......1750 GT Am.............

N° di serie { autotelaio ......1530001...................... Costruttore ...Alfa Romeo..........

{ motore ......AR 00551...................... Costruttore ...Alfa Romeo..........

Cilindrata motore ......1779.......... cm³ .....108,56...... cu.in

La costruzione del modello descritto nella presente scheda è iniziata il .... 19..... e la serie

minima di ......1000.............. esemplari identici e conformi alle caratteristiche qui riportate, è stata

raggiunta il ...31 luglio.............. 19.69..

Omologazione valida dal ....1.10...... 1969.. Lista ...69/7....

Foto A

Il modello descritto su questa scheda è stato oggetto delle seguenti estensioni d'omologazione:

VARIANTI			EVOLUZIONI NORMALI DEL TIPO		
Data ......1.1.70...... Omolog. N° .....2/1V Lista ...70/1..			Data ......1.1.70..... Omolog. N° .....1/1E Lista ...70/1...		
» ......1.1.70...... » » .....3/2V » ...70/1..			» .... » » .... »		
» .... » » .... »			» .... » » .... »		
» .... » » .... »			» .... » » .... »		
» .... » » .... »			» .... » » .... »		

Timbro e firma della C.S.A.I.   Timbro e firma della F.I.A.

SOSPENSIONI:

* 70. Sospensione anteriore (foto D), tipo   indipendente
* 71. Tipo di molla   elica
  72. *Stabilizzatore (avvitato)*   a barra
  73. Numero di ammortizzatori   2   74. Tipo   telescopici
* 78. Sospensione posteriore (foto E), tipo   ponte rigido
* 79. Tipo di molla   elica
  80. *Stabilizzatore (avvitato)*   a barra
  81. Numero di ammortizzatori   2   82. Tipo   telescopici

FRENI (foto F e G):

* 90. Sistema   a disco con limitatore di frenata
  91. *Servofreno (avvitato), tipo*   a richiesta
  92. Numero pompe   1 tandem

		Anteriori			Posteriori		
93. Numero di cilindretti per ruota		2			2		
94. Diametro interno		48	mm	1,89 in	38	mm	1,496 in
Freni a tamburo:							
95. Diametro interno			mm	in		mm	in
96. Lunghezza guarnizioni			mm	in		mm	in
97. Larghezza guarnizioni			mm	in		mm	in
98. Numero ganasce per freno			mm	in		mm	in
99. Superficie frenante per freno			mm	in		mm	in
Freni a disco:							
100. Diametro esterno		272	mm	10,708 in	267	mm	10,51 in
101. Spessore del disco		12,7	mm	0,500 in	9,5	mm	0,374 in
102. Lunghezza pattino d'attrito		77	mm	3,031 in	55,7	mm	2,19 in
103. Larghezza pattino d'attrito		54	mm	2,126 in	38	mm	1,496 in
104. Numero di pattini per freno		2			2		
105. Superficie frenante per freno		74	cm³	11,47 sq.in	40	cm³	6,2 sq.in

Timbro e firma della C.S.A.I.

MOTORE:

* 130. Ciclo   4 tempi
* 131. Numero di cilindri   4   * 132. Disposizione cilindri   in linea
* 133. Alesaggio   80   mm   3,149   in.   * 134. Corsa   88,5   mm   3,484   in
* 135. Cilindrata per cilindro   444,75   cm³   27,14   cu.in
* 136. Cilindrata totale   1.779   cm³   108,56   cu.in
* 137. Materiale gruppo cilindri   alluminio
* 138. Materiale canne (avvitato)   ghisa
* 139. Materiale testa cilindri   alluminio
* 140. Luci di aspirazione testa cilindri: numero   4
* 141. Luci di scarico testa cilindri: numero   4
  142. *Rapporto di compressione*   9/1
  143. *Volume camera di scoppio*   55,59   cm³   3,392   cu.in
  144. *Materiale stantuffo*   alluminio   145. Numero anelli   3
  146. *Distanza dall'asse perno al punto più alto dello stantuffo*   45,55   mm   1,793   in
* 147. Albero motore: fuso /fucinato   * 148. Tipo albero motore   integrale
* 149. Numero supporti albero motore   5
* 150. Materiale cappello supporti albero motore   alluminio
  151. Sistema lubrificazione: coppa a secco / olio nella coppa.
  152. Capacità: serbatoio / coppa   5,5   litri   9,68   pts GB   5,81   qts US
  153. *Radiatore olio:*   sì / no
* 154. Sistema raffreddamento motore   acqua
  155. Capacità circuito di raffreddamento   9,7   litri   17,07   pts GB   10,25   qts US
  156. *Diametro eventuale ventilatore*   300   mm   11,8   in
  157. *Numero pale ventilatore*   6

Cuscinetti:

* 158. Supporti di banco, tipo   a guscio sottile   diametro   60   mm   2,362   in
* 159. Testa di biella, tipo   a guscio sottile   diametro   50   mm   1,968   in

Pesi: (con tolleranze ±5%)

160. *Volano nudo*   8,8   kg   19,4   lbs
161. *Volano con frizione (parte rotante)*   13,1   kg   28,88   lbs
152. *Albero motore*   18,3   kg   40,34   lbs
163. *Biella*   0,740   kg   1,631   lbs
164. *Stantuffo con anelli e perno*   0,525   kg   1,157   lbs

Timbro e firma della C.S.A.I.

170

MOTORE CICLO A 4 TEMPI:

* 170. Numero alberi ad eccentrici ... 2
* 171. Posizione alberi ad eccentrici ... in testa
* 172. Sistema comando alberi ad eccentrici ... catene
* 173. Sistema comando valvole ... bicchierini

ASPIRAZIONE (N.B.) (vedere pag. 8):

180. Materiale collettore d'aspirazione ... alluminio
181. Diametro esterno valvole ... 41,15 ... mm ... 1,62 ... in
182. *Alzata massima valvole* gioco zero 9,6 ... mm ... 0,378 ... in
183. Numero molle per valvola ... 2 ... 184. Tipo molla ... elica
* 185. Numero valvole per cilindro ... 1
186. *Giuoco valvole a freddo* ... 0,475/0,500 ... mm ... 0,0187/0,0197 ... in
187. *Inizio aspirazione prima del p.m.s. (con il giuoco indicato a freddo)* ... 36°50' gradi
188. *Fine aspirazione dopo il p.m.i. (con il giuoco indicato a freddo)* ... 60°50' gradi
189. *Filtro aria:* ad olio / a secco. Cartuccia si / no.

SCARICO (vedere pag. 8):

195. Materiale collettore di scarico ... ghisa
196. Diametro esterno valvole ... 37,2 ... mm ... 1,465 ... in
197. *Alzata massima valvole* gioco zero 9,6 ... mm ... 0,378 ... in
198. Numero molle per valvola ... 2 ... 199. Tipo molla ... elica
* 200. Numero valvole per cilindro ... 1
201. *Giuoco valvole a freddo* ... 0,525/0,550 ... mm ... 0,0207/0,02165 ... in
202. *Inizio scarico prima del p.m.i. (con il giuoco indicato a freddo)* ... 54°10' gradi
203. *Fine scarico dopo il p.m.s. (con il giuoco indicato a freddo)* ... 30°10' gradi

CARBURAZIONE (foto N):

210. Numero di carburatori ... 211. *Tipo*
212. *Marca* ... 213. *Modello*
214. Numero condotti per carburatore
215. Diametro condotto / condotti all'uscita del carburatore ... mm ... in
216. A seconda del tipo di carburatore: diametro minimo del diffusore / dei diffusori; dimensioni dei passaggio miscela nel punto di minima sezione con stantuffino di regolazione al punto più alto (esempio: carburatori SU) ... mm ... in

N.B. - I dati riguardanti i motori a due tempi e sovralimentati sono riportati nelle pagine supplementari.

Timbro e firma della C.S.A.I.

INIEZIONE (se prevista):

220. Marca pompa ... SPICA
221. Numero stantuffi ... 4
222. *Modello e tipo pompa* AIBB.4C.S.75 a stantuffi a portata variabile
223. Numero totale iniettori ... 4
224. Sistemazione iniettori ... nei condotti di aspirazione
225. *Diametro condotto d'alimentazione nel punto di sezione minima* ... 32 ... mm ... 1,259 ... in

ACCESSORI DEL MOTORE:

230. *Pompa carburante:* elettrica
231. Numero pompe ... 1
232. Sistema accensione, tipo ... a spinterogeno
233. Numero distributori ... 1
234. Numero bobine ... 1
235. Numero candele per cilindro ... 1
236. *Generatore, tipo:* alternatore ... Numero ... 1
237. Sistema di comando ... a cinghia
238. Tensione ... 12 ... volt
239. Numero batterie ... 1
240. Sistemazione ... anteriore
241. Tensione ... 12 ... volt

PRESTAZIONI DEL MOTORE E DELLA VETTURA (secondo i dati dichiarati dalla Casa costruttrice):

250. *Potenza del motore* 132 ... Cv (¹) SAE a 5.500 giri/min
251. *Regime massimo* ... giri/min ... *Potenza corrispondente* ... Cv (¹)
252. *Coppia massima* 19 kgm SAE a 3.000 giri/min
253. *Velocità massima della vettura* 190 km/h 118 miglia/h

255.
Eccentrico d'aspirazione:
S = 23,2 mm 0,914 in
T = 13,6 mm 0,536 in
U = 27,57 mm 1,08 in

Eccentrico di scarico:
S = 23,2 mm 0,914 in
T = 13,6 mm 0,536 in
U = 27,57 mm 1,08 in

R = Centro albero ad eccentrici.

(¹) Precisare se CV DIN, SAE, ecc.

Timbro e firma della C.S.A.I.

Disegno o foto luci condotti d'aspirazione, lato testa cilindri.

Indicare la scala o le dimensioni, e le tolleranze di lavorazione.

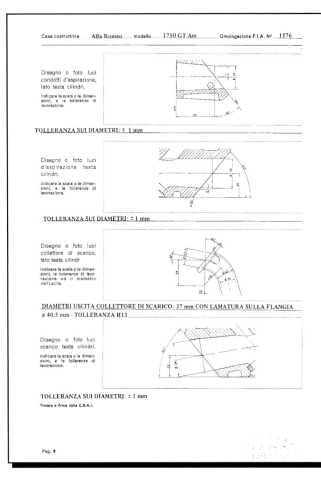

TOLLERANZA SUI DIAMETRI: ± 1 mm

Disegno o foto luci d'aspirazione testa cilindri.

Indicare la scala o le dimensioni, e le tolleranze di lavorazione.

TOLLERANZA SUI DIAMETRI: ± 1 mm

Disegno o foto luci collettore di scarico, lato testa cilindr

Indicare la scala o le dimensioni, le tolleranze di lavorazione ed il diametro dell'uscita.

DIAMETRI USCITA COLLETTORE DI SCARICO: 37 mm con LAMATURA SULLA FLANGIA
φ 40,5 mm - TOLLERANZA H13

Disegno o foto luci scarico testa cilindri.

Indicare la scala o le dimensioni, e le tolleranze di lavorazione.

TOLLERANZA SUI DIAMETRI: ± 1 mm

Timbro e firma della C.S.A.I.

AUTOMOBILE CLUB D'ITALIA
COMMISSIONE SPORTIVA AUTOMOBILISTICA ITALIANA
FEDERATION INTERNATIONALE DE L'AUTOMOBILE

Scheda di estensione d'Omologazione
secondo l'allegato J al Codice Sportivo Internazionale

Casa costruttrice ... ALFA ROMEO .... Modello ... 1750 GT Am ....

N° di serie d'inizio delle   { autotelaio ....
modifiche (1) descritto   { motore ....

Data di applicazione delle modifiche ....19......

Denominazione commerciale dopo l'applicazione delle modifiche:
.... Invariata ....

La presente estensione d'omologazione deve essere considerata come:

~~nuova omologazione normale tipo~~   errata corrige

Omologazione valida dal ...1.1........... 19.70...   Uffg. 70/1......

Descrizione delle modifiche:

– la larghezza della vettura sull'asse delle ruote è anteriormente 1568 ± 10 posteriormente 1580 ± 10 con i codolini divenne anteriormente 1668 ± 10 posteriormente 1640 ± 10

   la largeur de la voiture sur l'axe des roues est antérieurement 1568 ± 10 postérieurement 1580 ± 10 avec les ailes devient 1668 ± 10 antérieurement et postérieurement 1640 ± 10

105.44.54.00 :/005.00 ailes AR   105.44.54.109/110.00 ailes AV

Timbro e firma della C.S.A.I.   Timbro e firma della F.I.A.

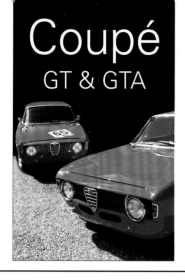

Coupé
GT & GTA

Appendix 8

Sales Brochure
Pages

Giulia Sprint GTA

Technical features

Cylindres	4 in line	Tank capacity	Imp.gals 10'/₄	**Rear axle:** anchored to body
Bore	mm 78			structure by two longitudinal

Cylindres   4 in line
Bore   mm   78
Stroke   mm   82
Cylinder capacity   cc   1570
BHP at 6000 r.p.m.   DIN   115
     SAE   133
Wheel-base   7'9"
Front track   4'3¹/₂"
Rear track   4'2"
Overall length   13'5"
Overall width   5'2"
Overall height
(unladen)   4'4"
Dry weight
(with tool-kit)   lbs   1639
Top speed   over mph 115
Tyres   165 x 14
Number of seats   2 + 2
Electrical system   volts   12

Tank capacity   Imp.gals 10'/₄

Carburetion: two horizontal twin-choke carburettors.

Ignition: dual, with two plugs per cylinder.

Valve timing: V-overhead valves directly operated by two overhead camshafts acting through oil bath cups.

Clutch: single dry-plate, with progressive engagement.

Gearbox: five synchromesh forward gears and one reverse. Floor mounted gear shift lever.

Rear axle: anchored to body structure by two longitudinal torque arms and rubber bushes; transverse anchorage is by means of a reaction bracket with rubber bushes on the frame and axle: the final drive is of hypoid type.

Front suspension: independent front wheel suspension secured to the frame by inclined transverse wishbones; coil springs and telescopic hydraulic double-acting shock-absorbers; transverse antiroll bar.

Rear suspension: coil springs and coaxially mounted telescopic hydraulic double-acting shock-absorbers.

Steering: re-circulating ball or worm and roller.

Brakes: 4 discs; the two rear brakes have the cylinder separate from the calipers. Mechanically operated hand-brake.

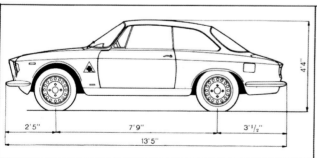 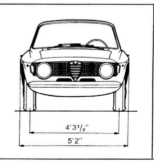 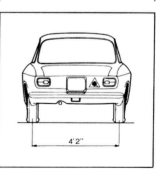

Specification of the 1600 Giulia Sprint GTA as shown in a 1965/66 sales brochure which also featured a similar table for the standard Giulia GT.

173

Giulia GTA
a competition Sprint

Despite appearances, a far reaching evolution lies behind the production of the new Giulia Sprint GTA. Externally, the only difference from the GT is the famous clover leaf, emblem of the racing Alfas, but as the name indicates (A stands for Alleggerita, which means lightened) the GTA is a vehicle that stands out by virtue of its performance. For normal road use, the GTA will appeal particularly to those who are active participants in the field of motor sports.

Revue Automobile

The engine of the Giulia Sprint GTA develops a 115 bhp DIN at 6000 rpm (133 bhp SAE). This gives the car exceptional acceleration and a maximum speed of more than 185 kph. Without renouncing any of the advantages of the GT, important reductions have been made to the weight

f the GTA by the use of special material and special methods. The reduction in weight is considerable and obviously increases the acceleration characteristics of the vehicle. The following important innovations should be noted: Special electrical system with twin ignition; Increased size of the carburet-tors; Newly designed induction ports and exhaust manifold; Completely new cylinder head to take the twin plugs; Sodium filled exhaust valves of greater dimension; A double electrical fuel pump; Close ratio gears in the 5 speed box; Availability (on special request) of an oil cooler; Magnesium alloy wheels of larger section and smaller diameter; 14" tyres of larger section;

Auto Sprint

Since we know of the ability of the Alfa Romeo design engineers to improve their engines, we can well believe that the power of the GTA easily exceeds 150 bhp, producing a very high power to weight ratio in the region of 5 kgm per bhp. Added to its road holding and manoeuvreability this makes the GTA an adversary to be feared not only in its own category but also by any car in the "Touring" class.

L'Equipe

A page from a GT Junior 1.6 sales brochure of 1972 demonstrating the Giulia's motor racing prowess.

Alfa Romeo take part – and always have done – in hundreds of races every year, and every race confirms the high quality of the company's vehicles.
Both the Giulia Super and the GT/Am, whose structure and style are identical to the GT Junior, have competed highly successfully over the last few years in both road and circuit events. The following is a list of their victories, restricted simply to national and international championships.
It is important to underline that all the winning vehicles are not special prototypes but production models. The experience gained with them can thus be applied at once to the production line.

1967
EUROPEAN ROAD CHALLENGE CUP (A. de Adamich)
EUROPEAN MOUNTAIN ROAD CHAMPIONSHIP (I. Giunti)
AUSTRALIAN NEW SOUTH WALES RALLY CHAMPIONSHIP (Chivas-Adcock)
BRAZILIAN MOUNTAIN ROAD CHAMPIONSHIP (E. Zambello)
BELGIAN ROAD SPEED CHAMPIONSHIP (S. Trosch)
FRENCH RALLY AND HILL-CLIMBING TROPHY
GERMAN ROAD SPEED CHAMPIONSHIP (H. Schulze)
GREEK ROAD SPEED CHAMPIONSHIP (« Mavros »)
ITALIAN 1600 cc SALOON TROPHY (« Riccardone »)
SOUTH AFRICAN STANDARD PRODUCTION VEHICLE CHAMPIONSHIP (Van Rooyen)
U.S.A. 2000 cc SEDAN CARS CHAMPIONSHIP (V. Provenzano)

1968
C.S.A.I. 1600 cc G.T. CUP (L. Cecchini)
MOUNTAIN SPORT TROPHY (Bardelli)
GERMAN SPEED CHAMPIONSHIP (H. Schulze)
AUSTRALIAN CHAMPIONSHIP (K. Bartlett)
BELGIAN ROAD CHAMPIONSHIP (J. Desmoulin)
BELGIAN LADIES' CHAMPIONSHIP (Christine)
AUSTRIAN ROAD CHAMPIONSHIP (K. Reisch)
BRAZILIAN ROAD CHAMPIONSHIP (F. Lameirão)
DUTCH 1300/1600 cc ROAD CHAMPIONSHIP (N. Chiotakis)

1969
EUROPEAN ROAD CHALLENGE CUP DIVISION II
— 1600 cc Class (S. Dini)
— 1300 cc Class (E. Pinto)
REPUBLIC OF CZECHOSLOVAKIA CHAMPIONSHIP (D. Welimsky)

SOUTH PACIFIC DIVISIONAL UNITED STATES CHAMPIONSHIP (J. Kline)
S.C.C.A. UNITED STATES' DRIVERS' CHAMPIONSHIP
— Production model Class G (P. Spruell)
— Sedan Class C (H. Theodoracopoulos)
BRAZILIAN CHAMPIONSHIP (M. Fernandes and F. Terra Schmit)
RUMANIAN CHAMPIONSHIP (F. Hainarosie)
ITALIAN 1300 cc SALOON TROPHY (« Ghigo »)
ITALIAN 1600 cc SALOON TROPHY (L. Cecchini)

1970
EUROPEAN ROAD CHAMPIONSHIP (T. Hezemans)
DUTCH ROAD CHAMPIONSHIP (Akersloot)
TRANS-AMERICAN CHAMPIONSHIP for cars under 2 litres (Kwech-Midgley-Everett)
S.C.C.A. AMERICAN DRIVERS' CHAMPIONSHIP Sedan Class B (V. Provenzano)
BELGIAN RALLY CHAMPIONSHIP (P. Y. Bertinchamps)
BELGIAN DRIVERS' CHAMPIONSHIP (« Christine » Beckers)
ITALIAN NATIONAL SPECIAL SALOON TROPHY
— 1300 cc Class (L. Colzani)
— 2000 cc Class (P. De Leonibus)
ITALIAN NATIONAL SPECIAL G.T. TROPHY (L. Cabella)
URUGUAYAN RALLY CHAMPIONSHIP (F. West-C. Assadourian)
CZECHOSLOVAKIAN NATIONAL CHAMPIONSHIP (J. Rosicky)

1971
EUROPEAN ROAD CHAMPIONSHIP (G. Picchi)
AUSTRIAN SPECIAL ROAD CHAMPIONSHIP (K. Wendlinger)

AUSTRIAN PRODUCTION MODEL ROAD CHAMPIONSHIP (G. Koenig)
AUSTRIAN SPEED SPRINT CHAMPIONSHIP (W. Loeffelmann)
BELGIAN ROAD DRIVERS' CHAMPIONSHIP (J. C. Franck)
CANADIAN PRODUCTION MODELS CHAMPIONSHIP (E. Clements)
ITALIAN G.T. SPECIAL MOUNTAIN TROPHY (V. M. Randazzo)
ITALIAN OUTRIGHT SPECIAL ROAD CHAMPIONSHIP (L. Pozzo)
SOUTH AFRICAN MAKES' CHAMPIONSHIP
F.I.S.A. CHALLENGE CUP 1300 cc Class (V. Ciardi)
F.I.S.A. CHALLENGE CUP 1600 cc Class (M. Del Carlo)
ITALIAN SPECIAL SALOON MOUNTAIN TROPHY (M. Litrico)
S.C.C.A. U.S.A. DRIVERS' CHAMPIONSHIP
— Class C Sedan (D. Davenport)
DUTCH ROAD CHAMPIONSHIP
— up to 1300 cc Class (B. Van der Sluis)
VENEZUELAN OUTRIGHT CHAMPIONSHIP (G. Spadaro)
SOUTH AFRICAN DRIVERS' RALLY CHAMPIONSHIP (Odendaal-Kuun)
C.S.A.I. CUP - Class 1600 cc Special Saloons (Zanetti)
C.S.A.I. CUP - Class 1300 cc Prototype Sports Models (Zanetti)

Details, descriptions and illustrations are for information purposes only, as the products may vary for any reason, including constructional requirements.
Alfa Romeo reserves the right to modify its products in any way. Some of the items described or shown in this brochure are optional. For information about optional extras, please consult our local price list.
Realizzazione CBC, Milano.
Printed in Italy. 72 7 C 101 ILTE - Torino

Giulia GT Veloce and Spider Veloce sales brochure from the seventies.

Alfa Romeo **2000** GT Veloce / Spider Veloce

Alfa Romeo GT/Am - 1970 European Champion with Toine Hezemans

For well over half a century, Alfa Romeo cars have been participating annually in motor-racing events and it can be truly said that each race is proof of their qualities.

During the last two years the GT/Am, side by side with the Tipo 33/3, has been a leading contributor to Alfa Romeo victories. In additio[n] to gaining several championships, both national and internationa[l,] in 1970 the GT/Am was the car in which Toine Hezemans won th[e] European Championship.

The new Alfa Romeo 2000's were developed from the experience w[e] have gained with the GT/Am.

GT/Am Victories

1970

4 Ore di Monza (Hezemans)
Austria Trophäe Touring cars up to 2000 cc (Hezemans)
G P Budapest (Hezemans)
G P Brno (Hezemans)
Tourist-Trophy, Silverstone Touring cars up to 2000 cc (Hezemans)
6 Hr Nürburgring (De Adamich/Picchi)
24 Hr Francorchamps Touring cars up to 2000 cc (Pinto/Berger)
Zandvoort Trophy (Picchi)
4 Hr Jarama (Hezemans)
Erzherzog Johann Pokal Touring cars (Krammer)
Premio della Stiria Touring cars (Krammer)
Hill-climb Stainz Touring cars (Krammer)
Coupes de Belgique Zolder gr. 2 (Franck)
Hill-climb Tros Marets (Berger)
G P Paris gr. 1-2-3 (Larrousse)
Rallye de Lorraine gr. 1-2-3 (Barailler/Flavigny)
Circuit de Dijon gr. 1-2-3 (Larrousse)
Circuit P. Ricard gr. 1-2 (Barailler)
Ronde Cevenole gr. 1-2-3 (Barailler)
Tour de France gr. 2 (Pianta/Alemani)
Critérium des Cevennes gr. 2 (Consten/Todt)
Int. Adac - 300 Km Nürburgring gr. 2 up to 2000 cc (Schultze)
Int. Adac Eggbergrennen gr. 2 cl. up to 2000 cc (Schueler)
Adac-Spessart-Bergrennen gr. 2 cl. up to 2000 cc and Touring cars (Schüler)
Adac-Flugplatzrennen Neuhausen gr. 1-2 cl. up to 2000 cc (Weizinger)
Int. DMV Rhein Pokal Rennen Hockenheim gr. 2 cl. up to 2000 cc (Hessel)
Flugplatzrennen Schwenningen gr. 2 (Weizinger)
Adac-Slalom « Rot-Weiss Köln » gr. 2 cl. up to 2000 cc (Deussen)
Rhein Pokal Rennen Hockenheim gr. 2 cl. up to 2000 cc (Hessel)
Int.-Avd.Hmsc-Flugplatz-Rennen Mainz-Finthen gr. 1-2 (Schüler)
Adac-Bergpreis Schottenring gr. 2 cl. up to 2000 cc (Schüler)
Suedwest Pokal Rennen (Hockenheim) Touring cars (Schüler)
Adac-Taubensuhl-Bergrennen Neustadt/PF gr. 2 cl. up to 2000 cc and Touring cars (Schüler)
Flugplatzrennen Sembach gr 2 cl. 2000 cc (Schüler)
Rheinhessisches Dmv-Flugplatzrennen Mainz-Finthen gr. 2 cl. up to 2000 cc (Schüler)
Sauerland-Bergpreis gr. 2 cl. 2000 cc (Schüler)
Coppa A.C. Verona gr. 2 cl. from 1600 to 2000 cc (Zuccoli)
Trieste-Opicina gr. 2 (Cecchini)
Trofeo Autosprint (Zeccoli)
Bassano-Montegrappa gr. 2 cl. 2000 cc (De Leonibus)
Coppa Sila gr. 2 (Rosselli)
Cesena-Sestriere gr. 2 cl. up to 2000 cc (Rosselli)
Trofeo Bruno Deserti gr. 2 (Venturi)
Coppa Carri gr. 2 (Facetti)
Easter Race Zandvoort (Hezemans)
Race at Welschap gr. 2 (Chiotakis)

Hill-climb Camerigerberg-Limburgo gr. 2 (Hezemans)
1000 Miles Interlagos-S. Paulo (Diniz/Diniz)

1971

Rallye International Neiges et Glace Touring cars gr. 2 cl. from 1600 to 2000 c[c] (Balas)
4 Ore di Monza (Hezemans)
Hill-climb Galapagar gr. 2 (Barrios)
Coupe d'Albi du Printemps gr. 2 and cl. up to 2000 cc (Mauries)
12 Hr Interlagos (Diniz/Diniz)
Easter Races Zandvoort cl. up to 2000 cc (Chiotakis)
Coppa del Nogaro gr. 2 (Mauries)
300 Km Nürburgring gr. 2 cl. up to 2000 cc (Hessel)
Coppa A.C. Verona gr. 2 cl. 2000 cc (Colzani)
Hill-climb Frankenwald (Isert)
Coppa Piemonte A.C. Torino gr. 2 cl. 2000 cc (Zanetti)
Coupes de Spa gr. 2 cl. up to 2000 cc (Franck)
Bassano-Montegrappa Touring cars spec. cl. 2000 cc (Finotto)
G P Brno II div. (Hezemans)
Rallye International Feminin Paris-S. Raphael gr. 2 (Vallet/Rodt)
Nagrada Zagreba 71 (Strek)
Vittorio Veneto-Cansiglio gr. 2 cl. up to 2000 cc (Finotto)
Coppa Sila gr. 2 cl. 2000 cc (Zanetti)
Tolmezzo-Verzegnis gr. 2 cl. 2000 cc (« Petain »)
Trofeo Autosprint (Zeccoli)
10.a Coppa Altipiano di Asiago Touring cars spec. cl. 2000 cc (« Petain »)
Gedaechtnisrennen J. Rindt gr. 2 up to 2000 cc (Ertl)
Corsa al Colle della Maddalena gr. 2 cl. up to 2000 cc (Finotto)
Sarnana-Sassotetto gr. 2 cl. up to 2000 cc (Finotto)
Trofeo Petrolio Español gr. 2 (Barrios)
Salzburg gr. 2 cl. up to 2000 cc (Krammer)
Hill-climb Behamberg Touring cars gr. 2 (Krammer)
Hill-climb Alpl Touring cars gr. 2 (Krammer)
Salzburgring (Krammer)
Corsa della Mendola gr. 2 cl. 2000 cc (« Petain »)
Corsa al Monte Pellegrino gr. 2 cl. 2000 cc (Fichera)
Coupes Benelux - Zandvoort gr. 2 cl. 2000 (Chiotakis)
6 Hr Interlagos I cat. div. V (Diniz)
Rallye del Monte Bianco gr. 2 (Chasseuil/Baron)
6 Hr Nürburgring II div. (Hezemans/Van Lennep)
Pedavena-Croce d'Aune gr. 2 cl. up to 2000 cc (« Petain »)
Norisring-Rennen gr. 2 cl. up to 2000 cc (Struckmann)
Ascoli-Colle S. Marco Coppa Teodori gr. 2 cl. 2000 cc (Finotto)
Oesterreich Ring-GP Oesterreich gr. 2 cl. 2000 cc (Krammer)
Bressanone-S. Andrea gr. 2 cl. 2000 cc (« Petain »)
S. Giustino-Bocca Trabaria gr. 2 cl. 2000 cc (Cesarini)
Delux Rally gr. 2 (McKay)
Zandvoort Trophy II div. (Hezemans)
24 Hr Paul Ricard II div. (Hezemans)
Trofeo Bruno Deserti gr. 2 cl. 2000 cc (Zanetti)

performance and power bred from the racing GT Am. 2000 GT Veloce and Spider Veloce:

The new 2000 GT Veloce and Spider Veloce have a remarkable background, they are the outcome of the GT/Am, 1970 champion of Europe and embody all the experience of the 1750's. They are even more powerful than the 1750's and have the latest equipment for safety and comfort. They are most outstanding cars especially when compared with others in their class.

2000 GT Veloce

GT Veloce and Spider Veloce:

Performance:

The new 2000 GT Veloce and Spider spell power.

Here is the most important technical data:

☐ Maximum power: 150 HP (SAE) at 5,500 revolutions.
☐ Specific power: 76.4 HP (SAE) per litre.
☐ Power/weight ratio: only 6.9 kg per HP (SAE) (147 bhp per ton).
☐ Maximum speed: over 195 kph (121 mph).
☐ 1 km from standing start: 30.6 secs.

Everyone can make their own comparisons with the same data for all the other cars of the same cylinder capacity and they can even include vehicles of greater engine size.

Such a comparison reveals that the Alfa Romeo 2000's enjoy a very definite and undeniable superiority, one which becomes even greater if one takes into consideration the price of the cars.

Engine:

A characteristic of the new 2000's is very high resultes of torque and power, results which are obtained by means of certain choices in the design which are typical of Alfa Romeo:

Twin camshafts, with V overhead valves, ac ting through oil bathcups. The twin-camsha system, though more expensive to manufactu re, ensures higher efficiency of valve opera tion, with the guaranteed optimal workir conditions;

The hemispherical combustion chambers wit centrally located sparking plug ensure faste flame propagation and more efficient combu stion;

There are two twin choke carburettors, pro viding the correct fuel supply at all engir speeds;

The sodium cooled exhaust valves, derive from Alfa Romeo's aeronautical experience are designed to maintain correct temperatu within close tolerance, an important advan tage especially in the severe conditions of m torway driving;

The design of the inlet and exhaust manifolc ensures complete and instantaneous chargir and discharging of the combustion chambe

Safety:

The new 2000 sports cars are the most powe ful of their kind.

But is there any relationship between powe and safety? Is it true that one travels wit greater safety when one has a 150 HP engine In fact, when one talks of ships or aeroplane there is a tendency to confuse power with d mensions, whereas, when one thinks of mo torcars, power is normally identified wit speed.

In an Alfa Romeo, however, there is anothe absolutely inimitable way of expressing th power of the vehicle, and that is the abilit of the car to produce at any moment lightnin acceleration whilst at the same time providir the necessary mechanical structure to matc such acceleration as well as the instrumen to denote it. From this is derived not only th driver's « sense of security », so important constituent part of one's peace of mind in th face of modern road hazards, but also th

2000 Spider Veloce

best technical means of dealing with these very hazards.

Acceleration:

From as low as 3,500 r.p.m. the new 2000's are ready to give maximum acceleration: a maximum torque of 21.1 kgm (SAE) (152.6 lbs ft). Here is the key to all the marvellous power of these cars wich are the first to leap forward when the traffic-lights turn green, if that is what you want, but which, above all, are the first to show a clean pair of heels to the others on the road.

The 2000's never let you down.

In practice, those 152.6 lbs ft of torque are rarely used in their entirety, for the very good reason that only half that amount of power is necessary to keep up a steady 70 mph. But the other half is always there, in reserve, ready to be called upon in any emergency.

Structure:

Another aspect of the Alfa Romeo power-security relationship is to be found in the structure of the car. In the 2000's nothing is taken to excess, by which we mean that nothing is made bigger or heavier than is necessary. Everything is worked out exactly, keeping in mind the maximum performance of the engine. And wherever safety-margins are required — for example, in the case of the suspension and the brakes — these margins are bigger than is necessary for even the maximum performance of the vehicles.

At the same time weight is well distributed and this, along with the aerodynamic lines, contributes towards guaranteeing maximum stability.

The tyres are 165 HR 14's, suited to the highest performances; maximum grip is assured by using the classical lightened rear axle with which the GT/Am 2000 is also equipped.

An important introduction in these cars is the limited slip differential which is identical to the one used in the Alfa Romeo Montreal.

As long as the two driven wheels grip the road equally securely, this mechanism works in exactly the same way as the traditional differential. But if one wheel happens to be situated where its grip is diminished, for one reason or another (water, bends, ice, gravel), then the differential removes some of the power from that wheel and transfers it, to increase the normal amount of power, by as much as 25% to the wheel that is gripping the road better. The result is that the car benefits from an increase of power, which is also an advantage for road-holding. The brake-system consists of two independent hydraulic circuits, one for the front wheels and one for the rear wheels. The master cylinder, with vacuum operated servo, is composed of two distinct coaxial elements which feed the two circuits separately. A braking power regulator is fitted on the rear wheel circuit which balances the braking-action of the front and rear wheels according to the intensity of the braking and thereby prevents the rear wheels locking.

The large dimensions of the discs and the self-ventilating prevent any fading of braking-intensity caused by prolonged or violent use.

The principal advantages that derive from this kind of brake system are: maximum assurity of operation, minimal braking pressure, rapid deceleration and the ability of using gradual brake pressure.

Preventive and Protective Safety:

The new 2000's get their high degree of safety not only from acceleration but also from their road-holding and brakes, as well as from specific study and experience which reveal themselves in:

The degree of control that the driver exercises over the car and the cars' agility necessary in moments of rapid decision;

The large degree of visibility, both horizontally and vertically;

The careful positioning of the driver's seat and the various instruments;

The long-range lighting system with halogen gas head-lamps.

To these must be added the way in which the car reduces the results of accidents: the structure of the bodywork has been designed to protect the passenger compartment leaving the front and rear parts of the body to bear the brunt of any collision.

The steering-wheel is dished and steering-box has been installed farther back to protect it in case of a head-on collision; there is no protruding part to cause passengers or driver injury either inside or outside and the upholstery has been padded to exclude such possibilities; provisions have been made for the installation of safety belts and headrests for the front seats (headrests incorporated into the seat in the 2000 GT Veloce).

2000 GT Veloce

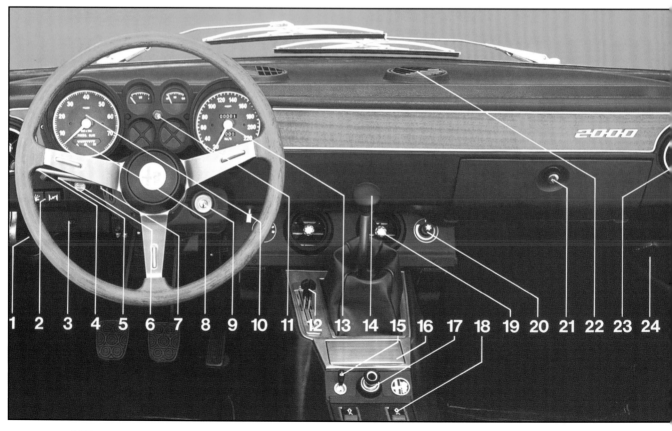

182

Comfort:

To increase passenger comfort without losing the sporting fascination of this car is one of the most remarkable achievements of the 2000 GT Veloce.

The 2000 GT Veloce is completely stable, i.e. it does not sway or roll, either when travelling along the straight or round bends.

The suspension has been thoroughly studied to give a comfortable ride. It is also extremely quiet.

The driver's position is a true cock-pit enclosed between seat, floor and dash-board: all the controls and instruments are within reach and easily read even at speeds of 195 km/h (121 m.p.h.).

The wooden steering wheel incorporates the horn controls and lights and indicator controls are on the column.

The bucket style seats are fully adjustable. As to their comfort, one should remember that they gained the highest recommendations in a scientific study carried out by two English researchers, Cyriaks and Watkin, who tested the seats of many cars for their response to

tomical requirements. Behind, the back is shaped to take two passengers. Such a h travelling comfort is naturally enhanced a two-speed heating and ventilating system by a large boot.

Windscreen washers/wipers
Choke and hand throttle
Fuse box
Exterior lights and flasher control
Direction indicators control
Heated rear window switch and warning light
Instrument lights switch
Oil pressure gauge
Ignition switch and steering lock
Rev counter
Petrol gauge and warning light. Minimum oil pressure warning light. Side-lights warning light. Warning light for handbrake and brake fluid low level. Main beam warning light. Direction indicators warning light. Choke warning light. Booster fan warning

light. Alternator warning light. Water temperature gauge
12) Heating, ventilation and demisting controls
13) Speedometer. Mileometer (total and trip)
14) Gear-lever
15) Two-speed windscreen wiper switch
16) Ashtray
17) Automatic cigarette-lighter
18) Electrically operated window controls (optional)
19) Air-conditioning outlets (optional)
20) Air-conditioning regulator
21) Lockable glove compartment
22) Windscreen demisting outlets
23) Fresh-air ventilation outlets
24) Pocket for possessions

The 2000 Spider Veloce is designed by P[..] farina and is a marvellous combinatio[..] esthetics and functionality.

Its comfort is in keeping with its high pe[..] mance.

Its main merit is due to the stability of [..] car, both on the straight and in bends [..] then to the style of seats, which are truly [..] pable of making even the longest of jour[..] as pleasant as a short trip. Their absor[..] and flexibility is just right, with rigorous [..] tomical adherence. The seats are fully [..] stable and reclining so as to ensure an [..] driving position for fast motoring. Both [..] have headrests incorporated into the seat [..] behind are two moulded seats.

As for the instrumentation and finish, it is [..] actly what one would expect from a lu[..] car and from a first-class body builder.

Especially elegant is the design of the d[..] board and the steering wheel. The boot is [..] to contain the luggage which other spor[..] owners have to leave behind.

Finally, for a car which is a friend of f [..] air and sunshine, it is particularly impo[..] to be protected against rain and cold. Fo[..] first, the soft hood is perfect, and it is r[..] in one simple movement. For cold weath[..] specially designed hard top transforms [..] Spider into a coupe which is as elegant a[..] open version.

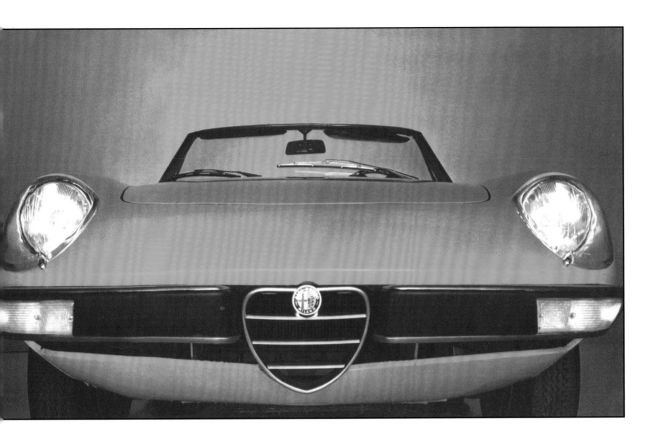

Alfa Romeo engineering means safety

Alfa Romeo can boast of many advantages over the motor industry in the rest of the world. Speed, acceleration, roadholding, braking: these are features that are found in every Alfa Romeo car, and in addition, low fuel consumption, silent running and comfort.

All this at normal motorway speeds, or rather at motorway speeds that are normal to Alfa Romeo's. These are features which, by getting the maximum efficiency from the vehicle and giving the maximum tranquillity to the driver, give an unparalleled degree of road safety.

An Alfa Romeo is safer, even at high speeds

An Alfa Romeo uses only half its power to provide speeds of 70-80 m.p.h. There is still plenty of power left for extra acceleration, even in fifth gear.

In comparative handling performance tests, the road holding of the Alfa Romeo has been proved supreme. It is a shining example of balance, calibration, weight-distribution and controlled suspension which has been achieved through 60 ears of testing and racing experience.

The braking power of an Alfa Romeo never deteriorates, no matter how violently, long or repeatedly the brakes are applied. This is due to the actual structure of the disc brake system, which is robust to protect them against deformity due to their main enemy: heat. In addition to this they are larger than usual and have a braking power regulator for the rear wheels.

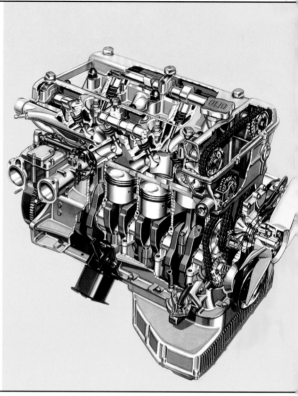

186

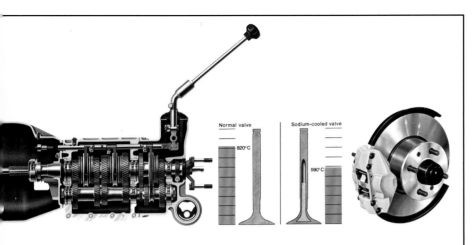

An Alfa Romeo gives more power from the same cylinder capacity

The Alfa Romeo engine has a 9:1 compression ratio. This is not exceptionally high, so the engine will last longer, in fact this ratio is no higher than most modern engines, but in conjunction with this, the engine gives a much higher power output for the following reasons:
The inlet manifolding is designed to give a smooth gas flow. So, the mixture is drawn into the cylinder instantaneously, completely filling the area.
The valves are operated directly by two camshafts without intervening mechanical components such as push-rods and rocker-arms, etc., which detract from the precision and continuity of the operation.
Similarly, ignition is instantaneous and the combustion total, because of the hemispherical combustion chambers with centrally positioned spark plugs.
Careful attention has also been paid to the exhaust system and to the design of the exhaust manifold. Complete and instantaneous filling of the cylinder area, total combustion and rapid exhaust relief: these are the reasons why an Alfa Romeo engine has more power per c.c.

This complete and waste-free combustion is, also, the reasons for the well-known fuel economy of all Alfa Romeos. The power of an Alfa Romeo engine is not, however, concentrated above 4,500 r.p.m.
It is evenly balanced and distributed over the whole range of engine speeds, and it is backed up by a 5-speed gearbox with carefully spaced ratios.
Therefore, not only is an Alfa Romeo capable of reaching very high speeds, but it is capable of reaching them extremely quickly. It can accelerate away first at traffic lights and overtake easily and without risk.
The 5th gear is another special Alfa Romeo feature, because it is not an 'added' gear like an overdrive.
Naturally it can save fuel on motorway cruising: but it is above all a proper gear with real acceleration powers, designed for modern motoring requirements where acceleration is needed even at high motorway speeds.

An Alfa Romeo lasts longer, despite its higher performance

The maximum speed of an Alfa Romeo engine is between 5,500 and 6,000 r.p.m. and the engine is under no strain even at these speeds. It allows the car to be run at top speed over great distances. It must also be borne in mind, that an Alfa Romeo can reach very high cruising speeds at only 4,000/4,500 r.p.m.
For smooth, vibration free high speed running the crankshaft is supported on 5 bearings instead of the usual 3. Finally, the only way to get the maximum power out of an engine, at all times, is to keep it 'cool'. Therefore:

● Alfa Romeo engines rapidly dissipate heat because the block, cylinder head and sump are made not of cast-iron but of light alloy;

● The cylinder liners are in direct contact with water circulating in the cooling system;

● The cylinder valves are sodium cooled to keep them at relatively low temperatures.

At Balocco, Alfa Romeo have their specially equipped test track.
There are winding roads, flooded areas and, of course, a highspeed track which extends for nearly 4 miles. This section includes straights and bends which are faithful reproductions of the most exacting ones from famous motor-racing circuits (Monza, Zandvoort, etc.). Thousands of tests take place here at varied speeds and under strenuous conditions. We test car bodies, shock-absorbers, suspensions, gear boxes and brakes, in fact all parts of our cars.
The Alfa Romeo 2000 GT Veloce and Spider Veloce were born on the track, but it is at Balocco that they have undergone those improvements which make them ideal cars, silent and comfortable for long trips.

Cylinders	four in line
Bore and stroke, mm	84 x 88,5
Cylinder capacity cc	1962
Power at 5500 rpm BHP (SAE rating)	150
Max. torque at 3500 rpm kgm (SAE)	21.1 (152.6 lbs. ft.)
Wheelbase mm	2350 (92.7 ins.)
Track, front mm	1324 (52.1 ins.)
Track, rear mm	1274 (50.1 ins.)
Overall lenght mm	4100 (161.4 ins.)
Overall width mm	1580 (62.2 ins.)
Overall height mm	1315 (51.8 ins.)
Kerb weight kg	1040 (2288 lbs.)
Maximum speed kph	over 195 (121 mph)
One km. from standing start secs	30.6
Tyres	165 HR 14
No. of seats	4
Electrical installation V. a/h	12/50
Tank capacity ltrs	53 (11.6 Imp. galls.)

2000 GT Veloce

2000 Spider Veloce

Cylinders	four in line
Bore and stroke, mm	84 x 88,5
Cylinder capacity cc	1962
Power at 5500 rpm BHP (SAE rating)	150
Max. torque at 3500 rpm kgm (SAE)	21.1 (152.6 lbs. ft.)
Wheelbase mm	2250 (88.6 ins.)
Track, front mm	1324 (52.1 ins.)
Track, rear mm	1274 (50.1 ins.)
Overall lenght mm	4120 (162.24 ins.)
Overall width mm	1630 (64.2 ins.)
Overall height mm	1290 (50.8 ins.)
Kerb weight kg	1040 (2288 lbs.)
Maximum speed kph	over 195 (121 mph.)
One km. from standing start secs	30.6
Tyres	165 HR 14
No. of seats	2+2
Electrical installation V. a/h	12/50
Tank capacity ltrs	51 (11.2 Imp. galls.)

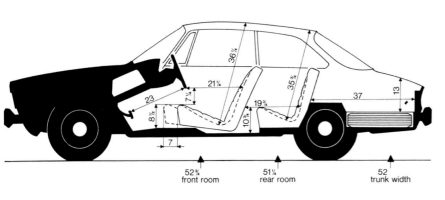

52¾ front room   51¼ rear room   52 trunk width

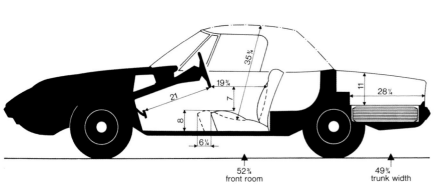

52¾ front room   49¾ trunk width

Carburetion: two horizontal twin-choke carburettors.

Valve timing: V-Overhead valves directly operated by two overhead camshafts acting through oil bath cups. Sodium-cooled valves.

Electrical system: alternator 420 Watt.

Clutch: single dry-plate with progressive engagement diaphragm springs; hydraulically operated.

Gearbox: five synchromesh gears and reverse; floormounted gear shift lever.

Front suspension: independent front wheel suspension secured to the frame by inclined transverse-A-arm; coil springs and telescopic hydraulic double-acting shock-absorbers; transverse anti-roll bar.

Rear suspension: coil springs and coaxially mounted telescopic hydraulic double-acting shock-absorbers; transverse anti-roll bar.

Rear axle: anchored to body structure by two trailing arms and upper-A-bracket for transverse anchorage, all with rubber bushes on the frame and axle.

Final drive: hypoid type. Ratio 4.1:1; limited slip differential.

Steering: re-circulating ball or worm and roller; dished steering wheel.

Brakes: 4 discs, dual system, brake regulator to rear brakes; vacuum-operated servo. Handbrake independent of main system, operating on internal drums.

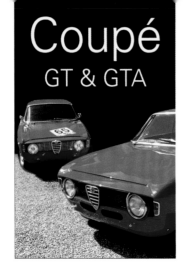

Coupé
GT & GTA

Index